E-Business Essentials

other titles in the Kogan Page creating success series

forthcoming titles

E-Business Essentials

Matt Haig

△△ KOGAN PAGE | *CREATING SUCCESS*

Kogan Page Limited
120 Pentonville Road
London N1 9JN

British Library Cataloguing in Publication Data

A CIP record for this book is available from the British Library.

ISBN 0 7494 3527 5

Typeset by Jean Cussons Typesetting, Diss, Norfolk
Printed and bound in Great Britain by Clays Ltd, St Ives plc

contents

the Internet and business

When the Internet began to be used for commercial purposes back in the mid-1990s, no one could have predicted the effect it would have on the business world. Web sites were viewed as optional extras that looked impressive, but didn't actually *do* very much. E-mail was treated with suspicion and considered by many as either an impersonal or an impractical way of communicating. Now, however, things are different. As millions of people around the world now use the Internet on a regular basis, any business worth its salt is expected to have a Web site and to keep in touch via e-mail.

Cheaper Internet access, ever faster and more powerful connections and the rise of the 'mobile Internet' have all played their part in the online revolution. The main factor, though, is the Internet itself: a vast network of information and resources that also allows people to interact with each other from anywhere in the world. However, it is not enough to recognise the significance of the Internet without understanding what it means for your business. We therefore need to take a closer look at how the Internet is used.

understanding the Internet

Succeeding at e-business is not a question of six-figure marketing budgets or technological wizardry. Rather, it is about understanding how and why people use the Internet. There are four main reasons for people going on the Internet. These are:

- to find information;
- to be entertained;
- to interact;
- to shop.

If a Web site cannot satisfy any of the above criteria (and many don't), it is unlikely to become a cyber success. If, on the other hand, you design your e-business efforts from the perspective of the end-user, you will be on the right track. This 'outside in' approach is the key to every effective site, from Amazon to Yahoo! Even if your online activity is only intended to support or supplement your offline business, you must be able to offer something of real substance, be it information, entertainment, interaction or fantastic products. Furthermore, although the world's population of e-shoppers is rapidly on the increase, online shopping is a completely different practice to shopping on the high street. For a start, nobody is going to just 'pass by' your site and make a spur of the moment purchase. People who arrive at your site are there because they have sought you out, not because you have an attractive workplace or because you are conveniently located.

Businesses are now expected to inform and interact with their customers at a closer level than ever before. The old business cry of 'location, location, location' has now been over-shadowed by the voice of e-business: 'information, information, information'.

Another difference is that you have a lot more competition.

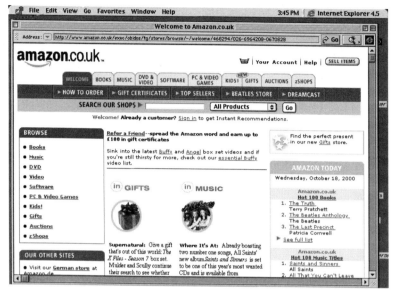

Figure 1.1 *Amazon: an 'outside in' approach*

While a record shop in Cambridge may be the only seller of rare jazz albums in that area, on the Web, there will be many other places people can visit to satisfy their jazz cravings. This means that simply laying out your wares isn't enough. No matter how 'niche' your business is, the chances are that there are other people out there doing something similar (for instance, there are over 100 Web sites out there selling nothing but hot chilli sauce). The Internet may have made the world a smaller place, but it has made the market a whole lot larger. You therefore need to add value to your Web site, and to differentiate your e-business from its competition. This is the challenge this book will help you rise to, by showing you how to tackle and work with the Internet on its own terms.

about this book

This book is intended to provide you with the knowledge needed to make a success of your e-business activity. Whether you are a Net novice or veteran, you should be able to find information that will help you harness the power of the Internet and use it to your advantage. Among other things, this book will help you:

- ▦ realise what you can achieve from e-business;
- ▦ clarify your e-business objectives;
- ▦ integrate your online and offline business efforts;
- ▦ decide how to develop your Web site;
- ▦ strengthen relations with your existing customers;
- ▦ conduct e-business research;
- ▦ make money online;
- ▦ market your Web site for free.

The main aim of this book, however, is to increase your understanding of how e-business differs from business practice in the real world. The unique characteristics of the Internet will be introduced, along with various ways to capitalise on them. This book also seeks to undermine the myth that the Internet complicates and destabilises traditional businesses. The Internet can add value to any business, old or new – all that's required is an open mind.

five Web watch words

To succeed on the Internet, it is important to realise that what works well in the real world may not work online, and vice versa.

The Internet is not just a new form of media – it brings with it a whole set of ground rules. These rules are centred on five Web watch words: speed, intimacy, communication, information and interactivity.

■ *Speed* The Internet is said to move at seven times the speed of normal time. It's expected that e-mail messages are responded to on the same day, Web sites are continually being updated and online markets evolve within a matter of weeks.

■ *Intimacy* Although the Internet is often viewed as cold and inhuman, it actually allows businesses to get closer to their customers than ever before. As Kevin Roberts, CEO of Saatchi & Saatchi Worldwide, says, 'people open up and share how they feel on the Net – something they just don't do in more classical research formats such as focus groups.'

■ *Communication* The Internet aids communication both between a business and its customers, and within the business. The convenience of e-mail and the accessibility of Web sites mean that employers and customers are less likely to be kept in the dark.

■ *Information* The Web is the world's largest and most up-to-date research library. You can find out more information about your competitors, your customers and your industry than ever before. At the same time, people will also be able to find out more about you. On the Internet – as in the *X Files* – the truth is always out there.

■ *Interactivity* Unlike traditional media, the Internet is highly interactive. One of the consequences of this is that people pull information towards them. This means that on the Net more effort is sometimes needed to differentiate your business from its competition. The Net's interactivity makes it possible for users to tailor information according to their own particular requirements. It therefore allows a business to communicate on a one-to-one level with all its customers simultaneously. Instead of broadcasting your message to the world in general, the Net enables you to narrowcast and communicate with individuals on their own terms.

doing business from the 'outside in'

E-business experts generally agree that the secret to online success is doing business from the outside in. Essentially this means that instead of starting with what *you* do and how you do it, you start with what the *customer* wants. The Internet is a 'pull' not 'push' medium. Users pull the data they need towards them – in cyberspace there is no successful way of pushing your business message on to people who haven't asked for it. 'Spamming' (the act of sending junk e-mail) is, after all, the ultimate breach of online etiquette.

As the Internet is a two-way medium, it enables a great deal of consumer feedback. Companies can interact with customers and discover what they *really* think about their service.

Net benefits

The time when the Internet was the preserve of desktop computers is now over as it can now be accessed via mobile phones, TV sets, even passport photo booths. As the dividing line between cyberspace and the real world becomes blurred, the Internet is increasingly seen as significant for businesses that have traditionally remained offline.

Although the Internet has the potential to make your business environment more competitive, it should not be seen as a threat. It is, instead, an opportunity to consolidate and build on your business achievements.

The benefits of the Internet for real-world businesses are clear. It can help in all the following areas:

■ *Saving money* The Internet can help your business save on the administration costs of taking orders by automating the process. E-mail can help you save on stationery costs, and online marketing often proves a lot more cost-effective than marketing offline.

▓ *Improving customer service* By increasing the possibilities for communication between your business and its customers, you can offer an improved level of service to your existing customers.

▓ *Keeping records of your activities* Because the Internet enables you to store information, you can keep track of all business correspondence very easily.

▓ *Attracting new staff* The World Wide Web is now one of the most important resources for job seekers. According to a survey conducted by the UK organisation Jobtrack, 79 per cent of college and university students say that the quality of a potential employer's Web site is an important factor when deciding whether or not to apply for a job there.

▓ *Preserving your market share* The Internet is not only a means of expanding your business, it is also a way to protect and hold on to the market you have already established. Real-world businesses risk losing out to slick start-ups if they don't embrace the Internet with open arms.

▓ *Making money* The Internet offers businesses new ways of making additional revenue. As well as providing a new platform from which to sell your products, you can also make money from affiliate programs, selling advertising space, securing sponsorship and various other methods.

▓ *Going worldwide* Your Web site can help you reach a worldwide market as geographical limitations are all but eliminated.

▓ *Being in constant contact* The Internet transforms your 9 to 5 business into a 24-hour operation. Your Web site works while you are asleep.

▓ *Knowing your market* As the Internet is interactive, you can receive constant feedback from your audience.

The Internet can therefore help you take market research to a whole new level.

more than the Web

When people think of the Internet, they tend to think of the World Wide Web. In part, this may be explained by the fact that the media's coverage of the Internet tends to centre on Web sites. The fact remains, however, that e-mail, not the Web, is the most widely used Internet application. Most people who log on to the Net do so either to send or to receive e-mail messages. In fact, it is possible to do e-business without using the Web at all. E-mails can be used to improve communications both within and outside your business.

The main advantages of e-mail include cost, speed and convenience:

- *Cost* You can send e-mail messages across the globe at minimal cost.
- *Speed* Messages can be sent and received within a few seconds, which is probably why e-mail advocates refer to the postal service as 'snail mail'.
- *Convenience* E-mail allows you to send as many messages to as many people as you want to, when and where it is convenient. You can also choose to receive and respond to messages as and when you want to.

Despite its obvious advantages, many businesses view e-mail as a mixed blessing. Because of its convenience, many companies suffer from 'e-mail overload', with mailboxes overburdened with messages sent to different people and departments simultaneously, as well as annoying 'spam' (junk) messages. The other criticism often made of e-mail is that it is all too easy for e-mail messages to get into the wrong hands. By empowering everyone within an organisation with the ability to contact anyone else (either inside or outside the company) from a business e-mail address, it has the potential to damage a company's reputation.

While there may be some truth to this criticism, the advantages of e-mail clearly outweigh the disadvantages. It's cheap, convenient and can be powerfully effective. Furthermore, it does not replace or jeopardise other communication tools such as the phone or fax. As Guy Fielding, a communications specialist at Oxford University, points out, 'E-mail is not destructive of other forms of communication. In fact, it probably has the opposite effect. It has more of an impact on *how* the other channels are used, not on whether they're used.'

This means that e-mail increases the value of other communications, as well as being an effective means of communication itself.

the Internet and the real world

Although to a certain extent the Internet can be seen as separate to the 'bricks and mortar' real world, the dividing line is becoming increasingly blurred. For a start, the Internet is no longer confined to the desktop. Owing to technological advances, it can now be accessed virtually anywhere, via TV, mobile phones, passport photo booths and car stereos. It is ever more difficult to ascertain where the real world ends and cyberspace begins.

Whether your business originated offline or online, it is now necessary to take a fully integrated 'clicks and bricks' approach.

the future of business

Within less than a decade, the Internet has grown from being an obscure technology used only by government officials and academics to what many have heralded as 'the future of busi-ness'. With phenomenal and unprecedented growth in the number of users, as well as the amount of information that can be accessed, the Internet has become the fastest-growing medium in history.

Because the rise in Internet usage has been so fast, it's real business impact has often been hard to assess. At the close of the last millennium, it seemed that the new breed of slick and shiny Internet start-ups would be the real winners of the online era. Traditional 'bricks and mortar' businesses were confined to the sidelines as the real world and cyberspace seemed completely incompatible.

The success of both large and small real-world business on the Internet, however, has brought about a radical rethinking of the significance of e-business. Many more companies are reaping real and substantial rewards via their online efforts. There are the big US names of Web profitability (AOL, Yahoo!, eBay and so on), but there are also thousands of small compa-nies around the world that have figured out how to make a profit. Equally, more established companies have discovered ways in which to use the capabilities of the Web to expand their businesses or offer customers better service.

summary

While the Internet is now universally recognised as being an important business medium, many business owners and managers remain unclear about what it can do for them. To gain this understanding, it is important to comprehend why, when and how people use the Net. It is also necessary to be aware of the wide business use it can be put to (as we have seen, this extends far beyond sales increases).

While this chapter has sought to set you thinking in Internet terms, the rest of the book is devoted to the practicalities of successful e-business.

getting started

Although the Internet is a fast-moving medium, the preparation involved in setting up an e-business should not be rushed. This chapter looks not only at the equipment and software you will need, but also at the activities that need to be carried out before you are ready for take off. These activities include choosing an Internet service provider (ISP), selecting a domain name, seeking investment and conducting market research.

what you will need

One of the ways in which the Internet is said to have revolutionised the world of business is that it has lowered the barriers of entry. In cyberspace you can open up a shop without paying rent for premises. You can put your company's name in front of a global audience without spending a penny on advertising. You can even link with other businesses to create, in effect, a worldwide sales team at no extra cost. However, while property, advertising and sales staff may be optional extras, there are some things you really cannot be without in the e-business era. First and foremost, you will need a computer.

a computer

Although the Internet is now available via mobile phones and the TV as well as the desktop computer, a computer is still essential if you plan to do business online. The Mac/PC debate is not really that important any more. It used to be the case that if you bought a Mac, it would mean that you could not use a lot of useful business-related software. Nowadays, most major software packages are Mac compatible, so this is less of a problem. Personally, I use an iMac, but this decision was based on aesthetics as much as anything else.

The main issue you need to consider is that of the computer's power. You will need a speedy computer with a lot of memory or, more specifically, random access memory (RAM). The more RAM a computer has, the better, as it will mean your computer will be able to work more quickly, support more software and crash less often than one with less RAM. Ideally, you should have a computer with at least 128 Mb of RAM.

a modem

You will need a modem to connect your computer to a phone line, and therefore the Internet. Increasingly, computers come equipped with internal modems, although you can still buy external ones. Essentially, most modems do the same job – the only way to tell them apart is in terms of transfer speed. This is how quickly data can be transferred into audio files and other formats. This speed is measured in kilobytes of information per second (Kbps). For business purposes, your modem should run at a minimum of 56 Kbps.

The word 'modem' comes from combining modulate/demodulate, which means the technical process of connection to the Internet.

a browser

A browser is the most essential piece of Internet software as it allows you to browse through Internet pages and download useful information. Without it, your computer will not be able to display Web pages.

In addition, browsers include significant extras, such as e-mail and newsreader programs. Microsoft Internet Explorer and Netscape Navigator are the most popular browsers available, and one of them is likely to come free with your computer or via your ISP.

a high-speed connection

A fast Internet connection is essential if you are going to set your e-business efforts off on the right track. The arrival *en masse* of broadband and asymmetric digital subscriber line (ADSL) technology now means that speedy and powerful Internet access has become affordable for even the smallest of businesses.

Here are the two main high-speed options:

- ▧ *ISDN* Standing for Integrated Services Digital Network, ISDN is available from BT and most other telephone companies. ISDN is, in effect, an extra powerful phone line that can be used for faster Internet access. It also means you can make a phone call and surf the Web simultaneously, using the same line.
- ▧ *ADSL* Like ISDN, ADSL uses an upgraded phone line. However, ADSL appeared much more recently than ISDN and is potentially much more powerful. This is because an ADSL line is *asymmetric*, which means it focuses more on data received by your computer (graphics, video, audio, software and so on) than data you send (such as e-mail and browser commands). This uneven upload/download balance

means that downloaded images appear much more quickly and also that audio-visual elements received are of a much better quality. As Net users both at home and the office tend to download more than they upload, the deliberately asymmetric nature of ADSL means there are fewer problems (more information on ADSL connections can be found at the ADSL forum on the Web at www.adsl.com).

choosing an ISP

To connect to the Internet, you will need to choose an ISP. An ISP acts as a 'middle man', providing you with the software needed for your modem to dial and connect to the Internet. There are literally thousands of ISPs out there and choosing the right one can be a nightmare. However, it is important that you think long and hard before making a decision.

An ISP has the power to boost or damage your business's reputation as it is ultimately responsible for how your site is presented. Before choosing an ISP, you will need to know how reliable they are, how quick their download times are (the time it takes for the Web site to appear on your customer's browser) and how effective their e-mail services are. If visitors to your Web site are frustrated with the service of your ISP, it reflects on your business.

When choosing an ISP, you need to consider the following points:

- ■ *Reliability* Ask if the company has a minimum downtime for repairs and maintenance. If they don't, be wary!
- ■ *Access* You will need to make sure the ISP you use has good access via the phone network (no busy signals or slow transmissions).

■ *Help*   Most ISPs offer a helpline service. Make sure the person you deal with on the phone understands and is interested in your business requirements. Check the helpline by phoning up with some questions. If the line is difficult to get through to or the representative is impatient or impossible to understand, take your custom elsewhere.

■ *ISDN*   If you use an ISDN line make sure the ISP you choose offers ISDN access.

■ *Newsgroups*   It is important to make sure that the ISP you choose carries all the newsgroups in Usenet.

More information on ISPs can be found at the NetBasics site (www.netbasics.com), an independent Internet advisory service. Another great ISP resource can be found at the following Yahoo! address:

dir.yahoo.com/Business_and_Economy/Business_to_ Business/Communications_and_Networking/Internet_and_ World_Wide_Web/Network_Service_Providers/Internet_ Service_Providers_ISPS_/Directories/

It provides links to international ISPs, as well as links to other ISP directories online. It may also be worthwhile asking the Webmasters at sites with speedy and consistent downloads which ISP they use.

an e-mail account

E-mail is a very important part of Internet business as you use it to communicate with your customers, suppliers, investors, the media and so on. In fact, it is likely that you will spend more time on e-mail programs than any other area of the Internet. You will therefore need an account that is reliable (sending and receiving messages on time) and convenient to use.

While many ISPs provide effective e-mail services, the e-mail programs that come with online services (companies such as AOL and CompuServe) are generally not very powerful, as they are aimed at consumers, not businesses. It will probably be worth your while looking at independent e-mail programs, as they offer some of the most comprehensive services. Here are some of them.

Eudora

The most well-known independent e-mail program on the market is Eudora, the grandaddy of e-mail applications. As well as making sure your e-mail messages are sent and received on time, Eudora also offers mail filters, enabling you to set up different mail boxes for different e-mail addresses, a spellchecker and automatic response tools. There is a free, stripped-down version of the program called Eudora Light that can be downloaded from the Eudora site (www.eudora.com). The full version of Eudora costs around £30.

Outlook Express

Outlook Express is Microsoft's e-mail program and is, unsurprisingly, one of the most successful out there. The main advantage of this program is that it fits very well with other Microsoft software such as Word, Office and Internet Explorer.

Powermail

Powermail is one of the few e-mail programs aimed solely at Mac users. It provides a comprehensive and powerful service.

other programs

A full list of every e-mail program is available at Yahoo! via the following address:

dir.yahoo.com/Computers_and_Internet/Software/Internet/ Email/

Make sure that the program you choose allows you to set up an unlimited number of e-mail addresses. This will ensure that you can create different addresses to serve different purposes, such as:

Info@mysite.com
Sales@mysite.com
Myname@mysite.com

your own domain name

If you want to be taken seriously you will need to have your own domain name. If you set up a site with a free online service such as AOL, Geocities or CompuServe, you will have to incorporate their name into your address. An example might be:

www.members.aol.com/mycompany

or even:

www.geocities.com/MexicoCity/EastSide/671855/mycompany. html

These names are referred to as subdomains. It looks far more professional to purchase your own domain name. Then your address might be:

www.mycompany.com

As well as looking better, it is important to get your own domain name for the following reasons:

- *it's shorter*   a short name is always going to be easier to remember than a long one;
- *search engines*   many search engines – most notably Yahoo! – discriminate against subdomains;
- *it's permanent*   if and when you change your ISP, you will not have to change your domain name if you own it – this is not the case with subdomains;
- *e-mail*   when you have a domain name you will also be able to have an e-mail account at that company, which means you will be able to set up straightforward e-mail addresses (info@mycompany and so on).

Of course, getting your own domain name costs money. You have to pay a Web hosting service to register it. However, with prices starting at around £40, getting your own domain name is a cost-effective investment that will benefit your company in the long term. To find the right company for you, visit TopHosts.com (www.hostfind.com) or Yahoo!, which has a list of hosting companies.

Think about the sort of Web site you will have before deciding on a Web hosting company. For instance, if you plan to sell products online, you should ask the company if they have a secure server (one that keeps customers' information, such as credit card details, safe) and if they have shopping cart software available, and at what cost.

selecting a domain name

If you already have a business in the real world and are looking to spread your wings in cyberspace, it is best to stick with the same name. Therefore, if your business is called Robert's

Records, you should try to purchase the same name on the Internet (www.robertsrecords.com).

You can, however, pay for more than one domain name for the same site. It may be useful to think of a keyword potential site visitors might type into a search engine and use this as a domain name. If Robert's Records mainly sells jazz CDs, for instance, it may be worthwhile registering www.jazzcds.com as well.

If you can't get the name you originally wanted, use your imagination. If the names 'Jazz CDs', 'Jazz' and 'Robert's Records' are taken, you could go for 'JazzJazzJazz' or even 'All That Jazz'.

Ragú decided to go for its own brand name (www.ragu.com) as well as a related term (www.eat.com). If you are starting from scratch and can choose whatever name you like, it may be wise to choose a short and easily remembered name ('eat' fits well into this category). You may also like to think of a name that will be listed close to the start of the alphabetical listings (Amazon and AOL followed this logic). It is also best to avoid names that tie you down to one product or service. Although Amazon started as a bookshop, the name Amazon does not tie it down to that category. Indeed, its it is equally relevant to CDs, DVDs and the other products it now sells.

Ira Bachrach, from naming company Name Lab in San Francisco, offers the following advice:

> You want a name that's invisible and imaginative because when your competitors are only one click away every little helps.

a domain suffix

A domain suffix is the part that follows your company name. The most popular domain suffix by far remains '.com', which was originally intended to denote a commercial or company Web site. If a person knows your company name but is unaware of your Web site address, they will probably type into their computer:

www.yourcompanyname.com

I would advise, therefore, that whichever domain suffix you prefer, you should also purchase the '.com' version of your address if it is available.

If you have a business based in the UK, it will also be worthwhile obtaining the '.co.uk' suffix. Other country-specific suffixes include:

.fr for France;
.au for Australia;
.nl for Holland;
.ir for Eire.

The other main suffixes you should be aware of are '.net' (for an Internet-based operation) and '.org' (for an organisation). The implication of these suffixes has, in recent years, started to diminish as more and more firms, including not-for-profit organisations, opt for '.com' addresses.

New formulations are, however, being proposed that are intended to be more specific. These include:

.shop for an online shop;
.travel for a travel agency;
.sex or .xxx for an 'adult' site;
.web for a Web-only business;
.store for an online store.

So, as well as your '.com' or '.co.uk', you may be able to add one of these to your shopping list.

seeking investment

If you are starting an e-business from scratch, you might need to seek investment. Here is a brief overview of the different sources of investment funding potentially, at least, available to Internet start-ups:

■ *Friends and family* 'Friends and family' refers not only to your network of friends, family and colleagues, but also to *their* friends and family as well. Amazon's founder Jeff Bezos kick-started his company with a hefty six-figure investment from his parents in the mid-1990s. They now own 6 per cent of the company.

■ *Angel investors* Angel investors invest in new but well-researched e-business ideas. They take an advisory role without making demands. They will be prepared to invest at an earlier stage than venture capitalists. To attract angel investors, you will need to have drawn up a very strong business plan and done a lot of research. Attend e-business networking events and have a look at services such as Garage (www.garage.com) that specialise in matching investors to start-ups.

■ *Venture capitalists* Usually these are big-money firms that invest a substantial amount of money in an Internet-based business, then work closely with that business to make sure things happen. Venture capital would provide your e-business with the highest amount of finance, but in return you would probably have to give investors a 20 to 40 per cent share and a lot of decision-making power. To find out more about venture capital funding, visit the First Tuesday site (www.firsttuesday.co.uk), which is full of advice and information on future networking events.

Advice on all aspects of e-business investment can be found at 3i (www.3i.com).

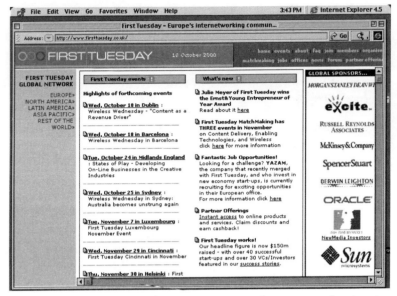

Figure 2.1 *First Tuesday is an essential resource for invest-ment seekers*

plan your objectives

Before embarking upon going online, you need to be completely clear of your objectives. Take time out to think about what you want to achieve online. You may run a business selling cosmetics, but that doesn't mean your site's only objective is to sell more make-up. When thinking about what your site should achieve, you need to step back and look at the situation from a customer's perspective, because on the Internet the customer is definitely in control.

Here are some general objectives that may apply to your site. You may want your site to:

■ increase sales;
■ build trust;

- generate greater brand awareness;
- offer improved customer service;
- provide relevant and up-to-date information;
- expand your business overseas;
- provide a point of contact for your existing offline customers.

When you have put together your objectives, you will then be able to clarify how you are targeting your prospective customers and how much money you should spend on developing the site.

market research

Before you set up online, you will need to conduct market research to help formulate your objectives. Online research will enable you to keep track of your competitors, potential customers and any other factors that could influence your e-business.

The Internet is the perfect research tool in that it can provide more information than any other source. To find what you are looking for, you will need to conduct searches via the major search engines.

search engines

Search engines convert online chaos into relative order. Without them, online research would be virtually impossible. You can use search engines to find information on practically anything to do with your e-business. The main search sites you should check out are:

- AltaVista at www.altavista.com
- Excite at www.excite.com or .co.uk

- Google at www.google.com
- Go.com at www.infoseek.com
- Lycos at www.lycos.com or .co.uk
- UK Index at www.ukindex.co.uk
- Yahoo! at www.yahoo.com or .co.uk

Figure 2.2 *AltaVista is one of the largest and longest established of the search engines*

To find information on who your competitors are and what they are doing, when at the Web site of one of these search engines, type the words you think people would use to get to a site like yours. Use as many different search engines as possible because each will bring up different matches. Try to find trade press sites as well as the sites of your immediate competitors. You need to find out how big your online target market is and who presently caters for it. Look at the strengths and weaknesses of your rivals and how their sites are designed. Are they easy to navigate?

Other things to look out for at rival sites include the following:

- *Adverts*   Do they have adverts on their site? If they do, it might be worthwhile going undercover. Pose as a potential advertiser and get them to send you their media pack. This will tell you how much they charge for advertising.
- *Newsletters*   If they offer a newsletter or other information distributed via a mailing list, sign up for it.
- *Interactivity*   Is interactivity encouraged? Does the site provide visitors with the opportunity to get involved and offer feedback?
- *The site's aim*   Try to work out whether or not the site is self-sufficient or if it serves to support a business in the real world.
- *Site traffic*   Look out for hit counters. Although they can be inaccurate (and, as a result, are increasingly unpopular), they do give you some measure of a site's popularity.

bookmarks

When you are conducting your research, you might want to make use of the bookmark facility available on both Internet Explorer and Netscape Navigator. This will help you compile your own directory of most visited sites. (The bookmark button is found on the Location toolbar.)

discussion groups

As well as exploring Web sites, you can conduct market research by using the search facility at Deja (www.deja.com). Deja is a collection of around 100,000 discussion groups that cover every topic from aromatherapy to zoology. Having a relevant keyword search here can result in very useful consumer research. You may also find people bad-mouthing your competitors. This will help you to avoid making their mistakes.

The following three sites all provide a mine of market research information:

- ■ *E-Marketeers* at www.emarketeers.com – this site is full of facts relating to consumer research;
- ■ *Cyber Atlas* at www.cyberatlas.internet.com – this service from Internet.com provides market research with a global perspective;
- ■ *Internet Sales* at www.internet-sales.com/hot/ – full demographic information for throughout the UK and around the globe is provided at this site.

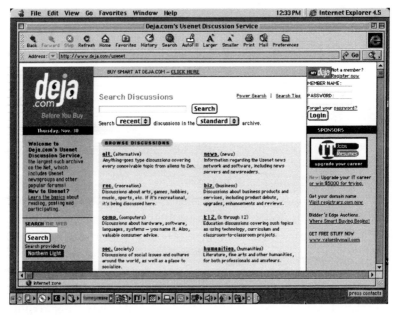

Figure 2.3 *Deja enables you to search thousands of discussion groups*

identifying your audience

Before you develop your Web site or plan an Internet marketing campaign, you need to clarify exactly who you are targeting. Although the Internet allows users to customise information for their own purposes, this information needs to be there in the first place. To know what to put online, you therefore need to know who is going to be using that information. For instance, if you are targeting audiences abroad, you should consider different language options, and if you plan to sell products on your site, currency converters.

You can differentiate between your various audiences by using the following criteria:

▓ *Geography*   Although the Internet is said to make the world a smaller place, cultural and national differences should be acknowledged if you are targeting an international market.

▓ *Gender*   You should decide whether your site is aimed at men or women, or both.

▓ *Age*   The days when the Internet was seen as a young person's medium are now over, as the rise in so-called 'silver surfers' (elderly Net users) has shown.

▓ *Net knowledge*   Distinguishing between Net novices and veterans will help you present online material in an appropriate way.

▓ *Company awareness*   If your business is based offline, you should distinguish between people who already know your business and those who will find out about you via the Net.

Another point you need to remember is that paying customers may not be your only audience. Competitors, the media, investors, job hunters and other information seekers may want to use your Web site, and should therefore be catered for.

summary

Thorough preparation is essential before taking your business into cyberspace. Not only do you need to make sure you have the necessary hardware and software, but you also need to be clear of your objectives and have a good idea of who you are targeting.

Remember also that no matter how prepared you are at the beginning, things can and do change. You need to be ready to respond to developments as and when they happen, even if this means changing an earlier strategy.

creating your Web site

When you are connected to the Internet and have an idea of your Web site's *raison d'être* you will be in a position to start building it.

If you want to create a Web site from scratch, you have three basic options:

- use a Web design agency;
- build a Web site using raw HTML code;
- use a software program that converts the HTML for you.

Deciding which route is best for you will depend on many factors – money, time and effort not least among them. Obviously there is no right or wrong decision as there are advantages and disadvantages for each choice. Outlined below is an overview of each option, to help you make up your own mind.

using an agency

Of course, the easiest way to build a Web site is to get someone else to do it for you. An agency is likely to have more experience of coding and designing sites than you, but, then again, it is also likely to be more expensive. It might also try to impose its ideas and ideals on your Web site. Before choosing an agency you should take the following steps:

- *Ask for references* Ask the agency for its client list and then approach the clients yourselves. This is how you will find the most objective picture of the agency's strengths and weaknesses.
- *Decide your budget* Have a fixed idea of how much money you are willing to spend on a Web site before going to see an agency. Also, make sure the agency quotes a flat fee, with no extra charges.
- *Know what you want* The worst thing you can do is go to an agency and say 'do what you want'. Much as the designers would relish the idea of being given a free reign to express their, ahem, creativity, they do not know your company or its customers as well as you do. At the very least, make sure you know the objectives you want to achieve and, preferably, what you want the site to look like.
- *Shop around* There are hundreds of agencies out there, ranging from slick operations with a large workforce to one-man-band set-ups. The Internet Works Web site (www.iwks.com) provides a comprehensive list of Web designers for you to look at. Some agencies specialise in certain types of sites, such as e-commerce sites, while others specialise in market areas, such as business-to-business.

working with HTML code

The cheapest option is to get to grips with HTML (Hypertext Mark-up Language), which is the coding that works 'behind the scenes' to put information and links on the Web. Contrary to what you might think, although using HTML can be tedious, it's not difficult. To build a Web site using HTML, all you need to do is write all the plain text, decide how it should look, then add the HTML tags to instruct the Web browser how to display text, images and links to other pages.

DIY HTML

Even if you decide to use software that hides HTML for you, a basic understanding of how HTML works will aid your e-business efforts by helping you to see how the Web is put together. For instance, you may need to amend your HTML code if you want all the major search engines to find you. Also a lot of the Web software products enable you to enter HTML tags directly on to your site, which will allow you to individualise your site to a greater extent.

Most browsers include a command that allows you to see the HTML code behind a page. In Netscape Navigator, click on View then Page Source to see how the Web page is made to look the way it does (other browsers have similar commands).

Here are the basic things you need to know about HTML:

- ▨ *HTML is a series of tags* HTML instructions, including formatting information and links, are provided in pieces of text called tags. These are labels placed within the text to give display instructions.
- ▨ *Tags work in pairs* To indicate when each command starts and stops, pairs of tags are used to surround pieces of text. For instance, if you want some text to be put in italics, it would be placed between the

commands <I> (meaning start italics) and </I> (end italics).

■ *Tags are written in capital letters* This is mainly to distinguish them from the rest of the text.

■ *Tags are invisible* Although HTML tags are responsible for how information is presented on a Web site, the commands between the brackets are never seen on the site.

the top ten HTML commands

Unlike a new language, where you need to understand hundreds of words before being able to communicate effectively, knowing just a few HTML commands can take you a long way. Here are the ten most important HTML commands:

■ <HEAD></HEAD> these tags are put on either side of the title tags at the start of a HTML document;

■ <TITLE></TITLE> the title tags surround a short description of the document, which is for your purposes only and is not seen on the screen;

■ <BODY></BODY> these tags surround everything that isn't included within the <HEAD></HEAD> commands at the top of the document;

■ <H1></H1> the first heading at the top of a document is surrounded by the <H1> and </H1> tags, while subsequent heading tags are given increasingly higher numbers;

■ <I></I> text to be displayed in italics is enclosed by these tags;

■ <B></B> the bold tags surround text to be displayed in bold;

■ <HR> standing for horizontal rule, this singular tag displays a horizontal line that is good for separating sections of documents;

■ <P></P> these tags indicate the start and finish of a paragraph;

▓ <A></A> underlined text to indicate that a hyper-text link goes between these anchor tags with the letters HREF (standing for hypertext reference) following the first A – for example, <A HREF= "www.website.com"> website </A>;

▓ <IMRG SRC> this is a singular tag that instructs the browser to put an image on the Web site and a file name is always included within the brackets to tell the browser where the image can be found – for instance, <IMG SRC = "Bud Pic.gif">.

These ten tags will be enough for you to make sense of the HTML coding underlying Web pages. They will certainly help you understand how the World Wide Web jigsaw is pieced together.

Although this information will give you a good grounding, to build a Web site using the raw HTML alone, you will need a more in depth understanding. One of the best online resources is *The Bare Bones Guide to HTML* (at www.werbach.com/barebones), which provides a full dictionary of HTML tags.

Web design software

Web design software enables you to build a Web site without having to learn HTML (the coding language of the Web). Although this software costs money, it is significantly cheaper than the average Web design agency.

All the best Web design packages on the market are referred to as WYSIWYG – What You See Is What You Get. This means that what you design on your screen will look exactly the same when it is transferred to the Web.

In addition, a lot of packages offer design templates, providing you with ready-made design features, such as buttons, banners and icons. Another important feature to look out for is 'Roundtrip HTML', which ensures that the site you design will work equally well on any browser.

There are many packages on the market, but the following three are, in my opinion, the best all-round choices:

- ▨ *Front Page* If every second is going to count when you are designing your site, this package from Microsoft is for you. Catering for the 'businessperson in a rush', this user-friendly software is, without doubt, one of the leading WYSIWYG packages. It is also available in a stripped-down format called Front Page Express, which claims to be even quicker.
- ▨ *Dreamweaver* Macromedia's Dreamweaver provides a bit more in terms of add-ons, enabling you to make your site look exactly how you want it to.
- ▨ *Go Live* Adobe Go Live is a widely revered package that matches creativity with technical competence. One of the reasons for its popularity is that it fits well with Adobe's other design packages.

Before you rush headlong into buying one of the above packages, it may be worth looking in your local newsagents. Free versions of packages about to be upgraded are often available on free CDs that come with magazines about the Internet and computing.

Once you decide which package is for you, stick with it as it can take quite a lot of time and effort getting used to a new program.

setting up shop online

If you are selling products from your site, you will need to set up a 'shopping cart' or 'storefront'. The reason special software

Figure 3.1 *The Dreamweaver Web site*

is needed is that, although HTML can create order forms, it cannot process the order. To enable your site to take orders, you therefore need supplementary software that can read and calculate information a user enters.

As the e-commerce revolution rolls on, the number of packages designed to help build online shops has exploded. While these storefront products used to be tailored towards the top end of the market, there are now types to suit every e-business. Although most of these packages will provide you with a functional e-shop, they vary considerably in the way they support your trading. The best offerings provide order processing, payment recording, customer account tracking and inventory control.

Here are some details of the most popular storefront packages. Prices for all of the products will vary according to your specific needs.

Shop Site (www.openmarket.com)

Shop Site is a Web-based product, which means that you don't have to install any software on your computer. Instead, you choose from a wide range of shop templates that can be adjusted to the requirements of your site. Orders are stored on the server and notification is e-mailed to the shop owner. The software supports a variety of payment methods and enables you to accept two currencies.

Intershop (www.intershop.com)

To set up a store using Intershop, you simply follow instructions, fill in forms, upload graphics and pick and choose the elements you want on your site. Intershop is available in three forms to suit stores of different sizes.

Figure 3.2   Intershop is a user-friendly shop in a box package

Mäestro Commerce (www.maestrocommerce.com)

Mäestro Commerce can help you build your entire e-commerce site and provides you with customisable templates. The site's step-by-step approach means it won't confuse e-business beginners.

secure server software

If you plan to have an e-commerce site, you will need secure server software. This ensures credit card transactions are secure. Credit card details typed into an order form will be encrypted before being sent from the visitor's browser to the Web server to take online orders. Although it is possible to take orders online without a secure server, many people won't place orders unless you have one. Furthermore, if you want to avoid the humiliation suffered by Powergen and Egg when the security flaws in their banking and customer payment services came to light, secure servers are essential.

the ten commandments of Web site design

Whichever option you choose, you will need to understand the basics of what makes a well-designed site. The following ten commandments are intended to point you in the right direction. Further advice is provided in Chapter 5.

navigation is everything

First and foremost, a Web site needs to be easy for visitors to find their way around. If a trip to your site leaves people dazed and confused, they are unlikely to come back. A simple way to make your site user-friendly is to obey the 'two-click' rule, which is that no page of your site should be more than two clicks away from any other page. A clear and straightforward home page with obvious links also aids simple navigation.

planning offline

Before you start building your site, it is a good idea to put pen to paper and work out exactly which sections and pages go together. A flow chart format is an effective way of deciding how to lay your site out in advance. Look at sites that offer a similar service to yours. This will help you think about what works and what doesn't.

be familiar

With over a billion Web pages out there, it is unlikely that you will be able to come up with a concept that is completely new. In fact, this may be a good thing. Web users like familiarity, they like to be able to recognise what they are expected to do.

less is more

'Information overload' is a fatal flaw of many otherwise effective Web sites. It is better to spread information over a few pages than to put a lot of text on a single page. Break text into short and succinct 'text bites' by using lots of straightforward subheadings. This will make your site more user-friendly.

consider different languages

Only one in five people in the world speak English, so, if you want to make sure your site can really reach a global audience, you should think about including non-English Web pages. If you believe that the money you could make from non-English-speaking Internet users is more than the cost of translating your site's content (which is quite likely), it is definitely worth doing. As the Web's global dominance grows, this is one way of differentiating your site.

get to the point

A commercial Web site should make its intention clear from the outset. The home page should include enough information about your site and company to let visitors know that they have found the right place.

avoid too many colours

The 'rainbow effect' created by using too many or mismatched colours should be avoided, as it causes your visitors confusion and eye strain. Two or three dominant colours on your site are plenty if you want to create a clear and tasteful brand identity.

consider download times

Lots of big or intricate images should also be avoided as they take time for visitors to download. Use spot graphics (small images) or images with minimal detail as they download quicker.

keep it simple

Extensive form filling can complicate the e-shopping experience. One solution, if you have the resources, is to store information (credit card details, customer preferences and so on) so that visitors only have to fill in forms on their first visit. While this tends to involve using expensive software, there are other ways to simplify the e-commerce process, such as isolating order buttons.

avoid 'brochureware'

Unfortunately, a lot of company Web sites resemble brochures. They present a glossy picture of the company without acknowledging the customer. Little attention, if any, is paid to the fundamental nature of the Web, which encourages interactivity and the exchange of valuable information. Visitors have to flick through screen after screen of dull and patronising advertising jargon before coming away completely unsatisfied. When designing your site, forget your company brochure ever existed. Instead, think of how to interact on a human level with your audience.

Web design sites

There are various great sites out there that provide help and advice on designing Web sites. Here is a small selection:

- *www.websitesthatsuck.com* This site aims to 'teach good design by looking at bad design', providing links to expensive and high-profile sites that fail to make the grade. It also provides you with a running commentary on just how and why the sites 'suck'.
- *www.moonfish.co.uk* This UK-based Web design consultancy provides lot of useful advice on every aspect of site building.
- *www.builder.com* Billed as 'The Site for Site Builders', Builder provides features and workshops on successful site design as well as links to helpful design tools. Whether you are a Web design virgin or veteran, this site will help you to work at your own level.
- *www.webdesign.about.com* This site has done the hard work for you, as it provides links to a wide variety of articles at different design sites.

▧ *www.developer.com* This is where you go to find out technical information as its content includes advice on programming and HTML. Although the information is aimed at technophiles, a lot of the articles are very accessible.

summary

Whether you decide to create a Web site yourself or get someone else to do it for you, it is important that you have an understanding of how Web pages are formed so that you can make adjustments at a later date. It is also important to realise that effective Web site design depends on more than technical competence. The way the Web site looks and is laid out will also have a major financial impact in terms of how many people will visit and revisit your site.

4

making money online

Whether your Web site supports your existing business or is a completely new venture, the chances are that you will want to use it as an extra source of income. You may be aware that many high-profile dot.com companies have yet to make a profit. Don't let this fact deter you. This has more to do with excessive marketing budgets than poor sales figures. As will be explained later in this book, expensive marketing is not needed to generate online sales. In fact, the real e-business success stories aren't always the multi-million pound dot.com start-ups you read about in the newspapers. They are often those sites that spend next to nothing on advertising and let word of mouth build up by providing customers with what they want or by using their offline reputation as a means of assuring customers online.

selling your own products online

The most obvious way for your Web site to make money is for you to sell products from it. Doing e-commerce from your site is fast becoming unavoidable, even if its main purpose is to support your offline activity. People are generally less worried about the security of payments than they were a few years ago, so e-shopping is an increasingly popular activity. Consumers now expect to do more at a Web site than read screen after screen of glib brochureware. Therefore, if you already sell products offline, it makes sense to offer online transactions as well.

products that sell well online

The three best-selling product categories online are (in descending order) books, CDs and computer products. Books and music perform well because the Internet benefits categories that need to catalogue large inventories. Web sites enable book shoppers to search for a specific book much more readily than they can in real-world shops. Furthermore, ordering a book or CD online is not too risky for the first time e-shopper, as the price is relatively low and delivery straightforward. Computer products fare well mainly because people who purchase large amounts of hardware or software tend to be familiar with the Internet.

What all three of these top-selling products have in common is that there is no real reason to look at or feel these items prior to purchase.

Products such as clothes, furniture and food – where there is a desire to touch or test before deciding to buy – inevitably do less well. That said, as more and more people are getting used to shopping on the Internet, practically every product category is feeling the benefit.

selling services online

If you are selling services rather than products, you may need to think a bit harder about the sales process. Whether you are using your site to promote a service offline or you are actually selling a service at your site, you will have to provide a real example of how effective your service is. Simply telling people is rarely enough. You may have to offer limited free advice or some other proof of your service's value.

becoming an online merchant

To sell products online, you will need to be able to accept orders paid for by credit cards. If your visitors can't use their credit cards to buy products from your site, you'll be struggling to make sales. Speed is of the essence on the Internet and credit card transactions remain the quickest and most convenient method of payment. Its not enough to expect people to send you a cheque or postal order. So, if your business is to take its e-commerce activity seriously, it should follow the steps outlined below.

acquire merchant status

To make credit card transactions, you will need to acquire merchant status. Without this, the major credit card companies will not process the orders. If you already have a merchant account for your real-world business, you will probably be covered (although some issuers insist on a separate account for online transactions).

If not, contact the company that issues your own credit cards and tell them you are going into business. Also, you should get in touch with your ISP, as most of them have partnerships with merchant account providers and so can give you a better set-up rate.

set up automatic handling facilities

The best way to take orders is to set up a transaction system that sends the details a user enters direct to the card issuer, so the order can be verified instantly. Although you have to pay for such facilities, this is the most secure option available and will therefore help to increase your sales.

To find out more about automatic facilities, visit Web Sockets (at www.websockets.com) or VeriFone (at www.verifone.com). These sites also offer software products that simplify the setting up process.

put it together

There are several options for setting up an online ordering system. You can:

- *use an ISP* many ISPs offer shop-building services at reasonable prices;
- *set up your own server* this will involve gaining Secure Socket Layer (SSL) authentication, paying for an automated system (such as those mentioned above), establishing merchant status and handling it all yourself, which is a very time-consuming option and so is not generally recommended;
- *buy an 'off-the-shelf' shop* you can build e-commerce systems using all-in-one products such as Click and Build (www.clickandbuild.com), which can help you build your entire e-commerce site.

Whichever option you choose, the main thing, as always, is to think about what the site user will make of it. The simpler the e-shopping procedure, the better.

selling advertising space on your site

Once your site is attracting a steady stream of visitors and any initial technical glitches have been dealt with, you may want to consider selling advertising space on it. Provided that you find advertisers that are relevant to your target audience, this can be an effective way of boosting your site's profit-making potential.

The most popular form of Web advertising remains the banner ad, yet there are many more ways to get advertisers on board. Here is a rundown of the main forms of Web advertising.

banner ads

A banner ad is an electronic band of text and graphics appearing at the top, bottom or, occasionally, in the middle of a Web page. The banners typically contain a link to the advertiser's homepage.

The main drawback of putting a banner ad on your site is that it will mean the Web page it is on will take longer to appear on a visitor's browser. From your perspective, the smaller the size of the banner, the better.

While banner ads remain the number one choice for Web advertisers, the jury is still out on how effective they are.

superstitials

Superstitials are adverts that appear while a Web page or site is being downloaded.

This is a new system and has been tried and tested with great success by a number of US companies. They have so far been used to promote cars, films and trainers. Nike claims that it received 12 times more click-throughs than it had done with its banner ads and that its site traffic increased by 50 per cent during its two-month superstitial campaign.

sponsorships

Advertisers that have a lot of faith in your site may be interested in a sponsorship programme.

Sponsorships bring in a lot more money than other forms of Web advertising because a sponsor is often involved at every level of your site. The sponsor will expect to see substantial branding of their company and may even want to contribute content suggestions.

Sponsorships are usually worked out on a long-term basis so, if you are considering attracting a sponsor, you will need to make sure that they are likely to add to the value of your site. You should put a sponsorship pack together (of about six to eight printed pages) that explains the appeal and focus of your site, as well as the various ways in which you would be willing to bring a sponsor on board.

You will need to consult a sponsorship directory to find out which companies have allocated sponsorship budgets. (In the UK, the most comprehensive directory is the *Hollis Sponsorship Directory*, which, unfortunately, is not available online).

attracting advertisers

The easiest way to work out advertising rates is to base them on the length of time an advert runs for. This will simply involve deciding the amount of space you are willing to sell and working out a monthly rate.

Then you will need to convince sponsors not only of the quantity of site traffic you have, but also of the quality (in terms of relevance to them) of these visitors, so that the spend is considered worthwhile for them. It is important to remember that advertisers are, by and large, more interested in a highly targeted audience than a broad, cross-section of random visitors.

advertising networks

To get advertisers on to your site, the simplest option is to join an advertising network. The way they work is simple. You register your site with a network, providing a complete site overview and specifying your target audience, then advertisers belonging to the network decide if your site is for them. The network does all the work for you and you will earn a substantial percentage of the cost per thousand impressions (CPM) that the network agrees with the advertiser.

The only catch is that once you have signed up to the network, you will have very little say over who can and who cannot advertise with you. BURST! Media (www.burstmedia.com), DoubleClick (www.doubleclick.com) and Ad-Up (www.ad-up.com) all run successful advertising networks.

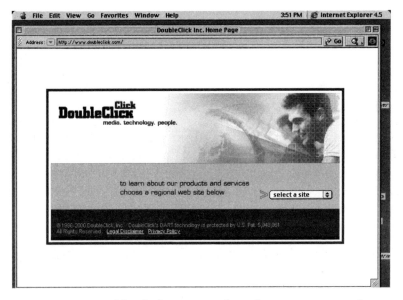

Figure 4.1 *DoubleClick is a popular advertising network*

affiliate programmes

A few years ago, online shopping malls were seen to represent the future of e-commerce. The idea was that Internet shoppers would be able to buy a wide range of products – CDs, toys, DIY products, computers – from various sites within one cybermall. The reason this was such a good idea, the cybermall advocates argued, was because it would benefit consumers by providing them with a one-stop e-shopping experience, while benefiting the e-commerce sites by bringing them passing trade. Shopping malls work well in the real world and can work equally well on the Internet.

That was the theory. What happened in practice, however, was somewhat different. While all the hype focused on the online shopping malls, a new way of doing e-business emerged: affiliate programmes.

This turned the idea of the shopping mall on its head. Instead of diverse Web sites being linked together to cater for the whole market, affiliate programmes joined similar Web sites together to sell the same products to niche markets.

Both the Davids and the Goliaths of the e-business world could soon feel the benefits. Companies such as Amazon and CDNow encouraged thousands of relevant e-businesses to sign up to their affiliate programmes, aiding their expansion and boosting the revenue stream for the affiliate sites. Now, online shopping malls have been left floundering, while affiliate programmes account for as much as 25 per cent of all Internet spending activity. Amazon alone has nearly half a million affiliates worldwide.

signing up to an affiliate programme

The benefits of signing up to an affiliate programme are clear. Sites receive commission without taking orders or delivering products. All this is the work of the site that sets up the programme and the software it uses. The only cost to you is the time it takes to find relevant affiliate merchants, link to them and then present them on your site in a way that is likely to lead to sales.

How much money you make from being part of such a programme will depend on the following factors:

- ■ *The commission rate*   The rate of commission in affiliate programmes ranges between 5 and 20 per cent.
- ■ *Relevance*   The more relevant the products you sell are to the content of the site, the more chances there are of converting site users into site customers.
- ■ *Site traffic*   Affiliate programmes are unlikely to bring people to your site, although they can add value to the sites content.

Although signing up to affiliate programmes is as close to being risk-free as the world of e-business gets, there are some important points that need to be considered:

- ■ *Take care when choosing an affiliate programme*   Make sure the merchant affiliate is reliable and delivers on its promises. The fact that you don't have to handle orders also means that you are putting the reputation of your site in another companys hands. It may even be worthwhile placing a few orders yourself before inviting your site users to do the same. Trust takes time to build online, and when lost can often be impossible to restore.
- ■ *Be realistic*   Affiliate programmes can and do make money, but they are rarely enough to support a Web site financially without other sources of revenue.
- ■ *You are a representative*   Affiliate partners are not offering their own, but someone else's products. To get people to buy affiliate products from your site rather than from the affiliate merchant itself, you need to

make sure they have a reason to do so. For instance, they will be more likely to click and buy a book about Feng Shui if it follows a well-written and informative article on the subject than if it is advertised in isolation from anything else on the site.

affiliate networks

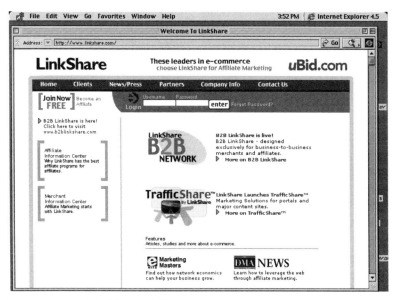

Figure 4.2   *LinkShare's homepage*

Affiliate networks – such as the hugely popular LinkShare (www.linkshare.com) – are used by site owners who want to sign up for several merchant programmes simultaneously. You enrol, then decide which merchants you want to incorporate into your site. The network then does all the work for you, tracking down all the different programmes on your behalf and sending out a commission cheque once a month.

The only possible drawback is that, by working for a lot of different affiliates at the same time, you may be in danger of diluting the power of your e-brand. Great care needs to be taken to ensure that the affiliate programmes add real value to your site. Affiliate programmes can only work *with* your site if they complement each other, as otherwise they start to work *against* it.

setting up your own programme

Rather than represent other sites, you may decide to get other sites to represent you. This option, however, takes a lot more time, money and effort. First, you will need to find Web site owners of similar or related sites to yours who may be interested. Second, you will have to take on the task of linking all the affiliate sites to your site. Finally, you will need to record and track sales to pay commissions.

Despite the fact that they can be difficult to set up and a lot of work to manage, there are manifold advantages to setting up your own programme. It will provide you with an array of sales reps that you only have to pay if and when they make a sale. It will also help you build a niche community of related sites, enabling you to reach a much broader section of your target audience. This is why more and more e-businesses are seeing affiliate programmes as the ultimate networking opportunity.

To find out more about setting up your own affiliate programme, visit Associate It (www.associate-it.com), which offers comprehensive advice on all aspects of this form of advertising, including how to choose from the hundreds of different affiliate software products on the market.

affiliate directories

Affiliate directories provide a mine of information for site owners wanting to sign up for affiliate programmes as well as for those looking to establish programmes of their own.

The directories enable you to link to sites that already participate in programmes so you can see how they work in practice. Some, such as the excellent Associate Programs site (www. associateprograms.com), hold their own discussion groups where you can ask questions on any area of affiliate programmes. One directory – siteCASH (www.sitecash.com) – rates sites on their ease of use, providing a comparative overview of the good, the bad and the plain old ugly affiliate sites out there.

summary

As the Internet increasingly becomes a part of everyday life, more and more businesses are reaping real results online. Customer curiosity has hardened into a willingness to spend online, with millions of people making purchases every sday.

To be able to capitalise on this, you need to ensure that you support your e-customers every step of the way. The next chapter will therefore look at how to make sure Net shoppers are fully satisfied with your service.

supporting customers online

Customer support is essential on the Internet, whether you are selling online or supporting offline activity. Buying a product from your site or making a return visit is an expression of commitment on the part of the visitor; this needs to be matched by a strong commitment on your part too.

Visitors need to have confidence in your site if they are to do business with you. This means combining professionalism with a genuinely personal touch. If you have an e-commerce site this is especially important. Far too many people in the world of e-business fail to see the Net as a means of deepening relationships with their audience, preferring to see visitors as 'hits' rather than as human beings. The companies that achieve real staying power and long-term success recognise the importance of information and interaction for Net users and subsequently use both to express their commitment to customers.

fulfilment

According to research conducted by Verdict, the main concern of the online consumer (and the potential online consumer) relates to fulfilment. Indeed, the main conclusion drawn from the research is that 'Excellence in all aspects of fulfilment will separate the online winners from the losers over the next few years.'

If you sell products from your site, you therefore need to make sure that your customers are more than satisfied with your delivery and fulfilment process. Here are some of the ways in which you may decide to do this.

- ▧ *Send goods out with receipts* Surprisingly many large e-commerce sites don't provide receipts, leaving customers with a bad impression of the site and its service.

- ▧ *Learn from successful sites* Amazon has a legendary fulfilment procedure. If you buy a book or CD from Amazon, you are taken through the ordering process one stage at a time. As soon as you have made your order, you are immediately sent a confirmation e-mail that tells you how to check on the whereabouts of your order at the Amazon site. Then, as soon as your chosen product leaves Amazon, you are sent another message indicating that your purchase is on its way.

- ▧ *Offer free delivery* The most effective way to satisfy fulfilment fears is to offer free delivery.

- ▧ *Show what products are available* All too often, shopping carts are left abandoned because shoppers go through the whole ordering process before being told a product is unavailable, often a day later. Make it clear which products are and are not available at your site.

- ▧ *Keep customers informed* If there are going to be delivery or other problems, make sure customers are not left in the dark. Send e-mail messages as soon as it looks like there will be a hitch.

- ▧ *Offer a choice of delivery options* Many online

shoppers will be willing to pay extra to have a next day or same day delivery. Customise the delivery process by providing a selection of possibilities. This also helps you to personalise your site.

▓ *Have a clear returns policy*   Successful e-tailers typically accept returns within a set period of time and offer to cover return postage costs for faulty goods. Publish your returns policy on your site alongside the main order forms.

getting people to buy online

While in the real world it is rare to see a customer literally abandoning a trolley at the checkout, on the Internet, where there's no one standing there looking at you, it is a much more frequent occurrence.

The majority of online consumers fail to hit the 'buy' button before they leave a Web site. According to some surveys, as much as 90 per cent of online purchases are not being taken to completion. This is why you need to support customers every step of the way. Here are some ways to limit the number of abandoned trolleys at your site:

▓ *Give full costs*   Consumers often get to the last step and realise that, with shipping, taxes and other charges, it's costing more than they expected. Make sure consumers are well aware of all extra costs before they get to the checkout (on the Internet, honesty is always the best policy).

▓ *Make the availability of goods clear*   The same rule also applies to the issue of availability. If a product a customer orders isn't in stock, don't break the bad news at the checkout. Make sure it is clear throughout the site if a product is or is not available.

■ *Add the human touch* Human interaction is an important way of getting customers to make that final purchase. People are anxious about the online shopping process and reassurance from a real person is very important.

customer research online

To be able to support customers effectively online, you will need to be able to understand what their needs and requirements are. The most obvious way to gain this understanding is to conduct customer research from your site. Effective online customer research can help you to:

■ direct your energies towards the real needs of your site visitors;

■ avoid wasting money on developing areas of your site that will not be visited;

■ develop a real visitor focus.

The sort of information that may help you gain a picture of your target audience could include the following:

■ *Age* How old is your average site visitor? Do visitors fall into a narrow age band or is it more of a broad cross-section?

■ *Gender* Are most of your clients male or female?

■ *Geography* It is important to know whether or not you are appealing to domestic and/or international visitors.

■ *Internet usage* Are your visitors heavy, medium or occasional Internet users? It will also prove useful to know what your visitors use the Internet for, whether it be to chat, for information or to shop.

■ *Interests* A knowledge of your customers' interests will, obviously, help to make your site more interesting.

To conduct a Web-based customer survey, you will need to add a form to your site.

Most of the Web design software packages enable you to create a form page by providing you with the essential elements (text boxes, radio buttons, tick boxes, drop-down menus, submit buttons) to transfer straight to your site.

If you are creating a form page using raw HTML, it is a bit more complicated, but plenty of advice can be found in *The Barebones Guide to HTML* (www.werbach.com/barebones).

If you want to conduct qualitative research and ask open questions, you will need to use text boxes. These are blank boxes into which visitors type freeform responses to the given question. If, on the other hand, you are conducting qualitative research and are asking closed questions (such as 'How much would you be prepared to pay?'), you would be better off using drop-down boxes, where visitors make a selection from a drop-down list.

In general, drop-down box-based surveys receive a better level of response as they require less work on the part of the site's visitors, who can fill in the whole form just by clicking their mouse. To make it even more likely that visitors will fill in your form, however, you need to offer an incentive. This could be either automatic entry into a competition or access to exclusive information. You could make filling in the form compulsory to gain access to a certain section of your site.

Flametree.co.uk — an online portal 'helping busy women balance their lives' – is one company that asks users to fill in brief e-questionnaires to build up consumer profiles by offering incentives. As a reward for their time, some users win a Flametree 'random act of kindness', such as a Shiatsu massage or technical counselling.

Figure 5.1 *The Flametree Web site conducts research by offering incentives for completion of questionnaires*

building trust

Trust is a necessary ingredient of any site–visitor relationship. It is especially important for e-commerce sites.

Becoming an Internet success is about much more than just attracting a large number of visitors. It is about getting these visitors to place their faith in your site.

It may come as no surprise to learn that the hardest task e-commerce sites face is winning over e-shopping virgins. When asked about building trust, online retailers always mention the importance of the first sale. As Jim McFarlane from PetPlanet.co.uk puts it, 'the issue is assuring first-time customers that we can be trusted. Once we deliver the first order without error or complication, the customer relaxes and starts to trust us.'

Harry Ganz from the UK's largest online pharmacy, Garden (www.garden.co.uk), supports this view. 'The hardest order is the first order: give good service on that first order and you have a customer for life.'

Here are some ways in which first-timers can be released from their inhibitions regarding the Internet.

third-party approval

Your site visitors are all in various states of Internet enlightenment. Some will already know that shopping online is safer than buying dinner in a restaurant, while many others will be very wary about giving out personal information and need lots of assurance.

Obviously it would be easiest simply to tell people how trustworthy you are, but you will need to make any assurances credible. The best way to do this is to sign up to one of the growing number of online reassurance schemes intended to calm nervous buyers. A good example is the Which? Web Trader Scheme (www.which.net/webtrader).

To qualify as a member, an e-commerce site must confirm that its shopping facilities are secure. Other reassuring logos that can build customer trust include those of the Truste Scheme (www.truste.com) and the Clicksure Certified Merchant (www.clicksure.com).

By getting in touch with these sites and participating in their programmes, you can assure your visitors that you're complying with certain Internet standards.

keep it familiar

One reason for the paranoia about e-commerce security is that the Internet is a new medium. E-commerce sites should be injected with a sense of familiarity and references to the 'real world' shopping experience. 'On the Internet, familiarity

Figure 5.2 *The homepage for the Which? Web Trader Scheme*

doesn't breed contempt', says Sophie Burke of Shoeworld.co.uk, 'it builds brand loyalty. With the use of recognisable icons, browsers are easily transposed from a traditional shopping experience to one that is online.' That's why most e-commerce sites have adopted the shopping basket idea, so that visitors can wander the online aisles, pick up what they want and then head for the checkout.

cut out the middle man

One important lesson many e-commerce sites have had to learn is that if third parties are involved, something can, and all to often will, go wrong. Don't subcontract out sales to companies that may not be able to keep to set timescales. The customer has trusted your Web site, not a courier service.

be human

The Web is often seen as inhuman and lacking the level of personal service found in real-world shops and businesses. People trust each other, not machines. As Yooni Suh, New Media Manager for Boxfresh (www.boxfresh.co.uk) advises, 'Start with the basic human emotions involved in friendship and the rest will follow.'

Good communication clearly helps businesses online to keep things on a human level. This is why effective e-commerce sites, from Amazon down, confirm customers' orders within minutes. If customers are kept in the dark about what is happening, they are unlikely to feel 100 per cent confident that what they have ordered will arrive on time and in the right condition.

Providing pictures of staff members and putting a real-world address on the site will also help to make it more human. Any company with a Web site should display their address and telephone number as this gives people confidence that the company has a physical presence as well as a virtual one. This is where clicks and mortar firms have an advantage over their solely Internet-based rivals.

e-mail support

While your Web site is a great way of starting relationships with your customers, e-mail is the best way to build on them. In fact, you may have found that e-mail starts to replace offline methods of customer support (telephone calls, fax messages, 'snail mail', face-to-face meetings and so on). It is fast, cost-effective and convenient and can help you keep in touch with people around the globe at any time of day.

However, as you may have discovered, e-mail has fast become a victim of its own success. Many companies receive hundreds of e-mails every day. Of course, if you become inundated with this quantity of mail, it is impossible to reply to each message personally. You may therefore want to consider one of the following two options.

- ▓ *Set up a file library of responses* If people are requiring the same information, set up a file library of responses to frequently asked questions (FAQs) and respond to each related message with a cut and pasted 'here's one I made earlier' response.

- ▓ *Use automatic response software* If you are finding a file library too time-consuming, you may have to consider obtaining an automatic response software program (your ISP is likely to offer one). You then set up different mailboxes for different types of messages and set the software up to respond automatically with a different reply for each mailbox. Response systems such as EchoMail (www.echomail.com) and Brightware (www.brightware.com) offer you ways to respond to infinite incoming e-mails as they arrive in your mailbox. A computer response may not be the perfect solution, but it is better than no response at all. Until recently, it was quite commonplace for e-mail requests and feedback to Web sites to remain unanswered or ignored. Nowadays, the software available enables you to preset criteria so that people receive a more personalised response than a mere acknowledgement of receipt.

These solutions, however, are not ideal and, where possible, it is better to send individual messages.

using e-mail wisely

According to a survey conducted by Internet research firm InTuition, 58 per cent of companies feel that e-mail can cause misunderstandings and damage business relationships.

The trouble is that as e-mail is such an immediate and informal medium that many people believe that an 'anything goes' approach is acceptable. It is not. When sending messages to customers or other people relevant to your business, you need to make sure no damage is caused. To do this, you and your colleagues will need to agree on some basic e-mail etiquette (or 'netiquette'). Here are the main business rules of e-mail netiquette:

- *Have a purpose*   E-mail messages must have a real purpose. Always ask 'Do I need to send this message?' If the answer is no, don't send it.
- *Use the Bcc: option*   When sending a message to lots of people simultaneously, use the Bcc: line rather than the To: or Cc: options. This will conceal the addresses of the other recipients.
- *Check the recipient's address*   An e-mail message that arrives at the wrong address can cause huge embarrassment.
- *Don't use emoticons*   Emoticons are icons used to indicate emotions in e-mail messages by resembling a face on its side; (:-) for instance is the icon used to express happiness). Using emoticons in business communications generates an unprofessional image.
- *Be grammatically correct*   Communications littered with examples of poor spelling and grammar clearly send the wrong signals.
- *Keep subject lines short and specific*   Ideally, they should be no longer than eight words.
- *Avoid sending attachments*   Many people can have trouble opening attachments and those who don't are often reluctant to do so for fear of viruses.
- *Avoid HTML*   Don't use HTML-formatted files because many e-mail programs cannot translate them.
- *Be brief*   Messages should always be fewer than 20 lines long.

▒ *Respond quickly* Make sure you respond to messages within 24 hours.

▒ *Be legal* Make sure messages are devoid of legally sensitive material.

▒ *Write in plain English* 'Please contact me if you have any questions' is preferable to 'Should you require any further information, please do not hesitate to contact me.'

For more on e-mail etiquette, see Chapter 9.

summary

To make sure you support customers online, you need to think from their point of view.

Fears about security and fulfilment must be alleviated by using your site to inform and interact with visitors.

The Internet can also be used to gain a better understanding of the requirements of your target audience. This knowledge can then form the basis of your customer support efforts, helping you to satisfy your site visitors on their own terms.

search engine success

The single most important way to ensure people notice your site is to get a good ranking on the main search engines. Most surveys claim that over 80 per cent of people wanting to find information online use a search engine to help them and that in a Web site's infancy as much as 95 per cent of visitors will arrive via the main engines. Certainly, if people don't already know a Web site's address or they are doing a bit of research, they are most likely to use a search engine to find what they are looking for. So, if your site isn't indexed with the major search engines, you are going to miss out on a lot of relevant site traffic. Despite the above being true, as the search engines themselves acknowledge, as much as 80 per cent of the Web is not indexed on the main search sites.

To reach the broadest audience possible, you not only need to make sure your site is among the 20 per cent that registers, but also that it ranks highly on search selections. As e-million-aire James Taylor puts it, 'A high search engine ranking is the best free publicity there is for any new Web site.'

keywords

Effective keywords are the most important criteria for achieving a high ranking on search engine indexes. Keywords are the words or phrases Internet users type into an engine to find relevant sites.

Your aim should be to identify the most likely keywords that will be used and make sure they appear in all the right places on your site. That is in the 'META tag' instructions (see below) embedded in your HTML code as well as in the page titles. These keywords will also be required when you fill in the submission forms at all of the main search engines.

finding the right keywords

Finding the words people would type into a search engine to find a site like yours can prove a difficult task, as there is often a limitless range of possibilities.

If you sell wine, for instance, you have all grape varieties and wine regions to choose from, as well as related food and drink terms. Remember to take into account the differences between British and US English if you are intending to attract visitors from both countries. If you sell theatre tickets internationally, have the US 'theater tickets' as well if you want to be found on both sides of the Atlantic.

META tags

Owing to the sheer number of sites on the Web, search engines have to automate the process of indexing sites. To do this, they send out 'robots' to trawl through the Web on the lookout for new sites.

As robots clearly lack the power of human thought, they rely on special instructions embedded in your site's HTML that describe your site and provide a list of relevant keywords. These instructions are called META tags and are enclosed within the HEAD part of your Web site's HTML code. There are two main types of META tags, the description tag and the keywords tag:

the description tag

The description tag allows you to provide a 15–25-word description of your site that will appear on search engine displays. META descriptions should, therefore, give in this number of words a general flavour of what visitors can expect from your site or page without burdening them with too much information. Take time to think of a good description because you will be able to recycle it for when you submit your site to the search engines (remember META tags are for when search engines come to you).

the keywords tag

The keywords tag lets you enter a list of relevant keywords for your site. You do not need to incorporate these tags on every page, but you should definitely add them to your home page and on main pages.

Here is an example of how META instructions are laid out:

```
<HEAD>
<Title> My home page </Title>
<META name= "description" content = "A description of your
    Web site goes here">
<META name = "keywords" content = "a, list, of, keywords,
    and, relevant, phrases, goes, here">
</HEAD>
```

To view a site's META tags, enter a site, click on 'Source', then 'View'. The HTML text (including the META tags) will then appear on the screen. A good tip is to look at the META tags of sites that rank high on search indexes to get an idea of the sorts of keywords and descriptions that work.

adding keywords to the main text

As well as in META tags and page titles, you should incorporate keywords into the main body of your text. Most search engines take into account the first 150–250 words of your site, so your home page should be peppered with the words and phrases you use in your META tags. Make sure, however, that the keywords you use don't look forced or out of place. Not only will this damage the quality of your site, but also search engines will discriminate against any site that lists keywords just for the sake of a high ranking. As Andrew Starling of *Internet Magazine* advises, 'Three mentions in the first 150 words is OK. More can be self-defeating.'

submitting your site

There are many sites that will submit your Web address for free, such as Submit It! (www.submitit.com), and several companies claim to be able to improve your search engine ratings for a fee. However, as each individual search engine uses different criteria, the best results are obtained by a careful choice of a title, effective use of keywords in META tags and by submitting your site to each major search engine individually.

submitting keywords and descriptions

Each search engine requires you to submit keywords and a description relating to your site and these can be of varying length. Generally, you are required to provide a longer description than the one you use in the META tag.

When writing keywords and descriptions, think about the words your target audience would be likely to type in to find a site like yours. With all keywords and descriptions:

- ▥ think like your audience and base keywords on benefits – 'value', 'relaxation', 'adventure' and so on;
- ▥ include your company name and each product or service you provide;
- ▥ use your top five keywords as the basis of your description;
- ▥ think of the people you are trying to attract and use language relevant to them, so, for instance, avoid professional terms if your main target is a consumer audience.

keyword help

If you are struggling with your keywords, there is online help out there. There are a several sites that can help you to refine your keyword selections. Good Keywords (www. goodkeywords.com) will help you find all the relevant keywords related to a primary keyword. For the phrase 'Web site design', it returns over 100 variations, each with the number of times it has been used in searches. When you have decided on your list, Good Keywords also creates the META tag for you to cut and paste into your Web page.

A similar service can be found at Goto.com. At this site, you can enter a keyword and find out which other words are most frequently linked with it in searches (www.goto. com/d/about/advertisers/othertools.jhtml).

submitting to Yahoo!

Yahoo! – the biggest and most popular search engine of them all – is the most important place for your site to be listed. In reality, it isn't a standard search engine but, rather, a directory. A directory is compiled by means of human judgement rather than a computerised 'robot'.

Whereas the term 'search engine' implies a mechanical process, the Yahoo! submission process is very subjective and based on human interaction. Yahoo! has a staff of hundreds of people who assess each submission and decide whether or not it should be included in the directory.

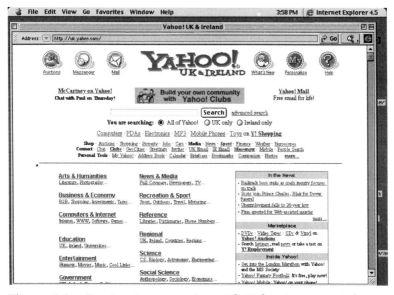

Figure 6.1 *Registering your site with Yahoo! is essential*

The Yahoo! registration process involves the following steps:

- Go to the submissions page.
- Type in the name of your company and its Web address.
- Find the category you want your site to be listed under.
- Add keywords that are comparable to index headings or topics. For instance, if you sell mountain-climbing equipment, you could list words such as mountain, climbing, sports, outdoors, travel, exercise, hiking, abseiling and so on. (Each search engine asks for a different number of keywords, but generally five to ten are required.)
- Provide a 20-word description of what your company does.
- Select the category you want to be listed in – Business_and_Commerce: Public Relations Agencies, for example.
- List your name and e-mail address.
- Click on the 'submit' button.
- You will receive confirmation by e-mail.
- List your registration in additional categories. This is especially beneficial if you sell multiple products.

One final word of advice: submit your site for easy Yahoo! categories, not difficult ones. It's far easier to get into a regional Yahoo! category than the main international (US) area. It's also easier to get into the personal page section than the business listings.

The submission pages of some of the other major search engines include:

- AltaVista at www.altavista.com/ cgi-bin/query?pg=addurl
- Excite at www.submit.looksmart.com/info.jhtml? synd=zbh&chan=home&sku=ls02&page=form
- HotBot at www.hotbot.com/addurl.asp
- Lycos at www.lycos.com/addasite.html

For a comprehensive list of search engines, visit The Web Site Top 100 at www.mmgco.com/top100.html.

beyond keywords

Search engine success is not simply a question of keywords and site descriptions. Anyone who depends solely on META tags, for instance, is going to end up sorely disappointed. Here are some other ways in which to harness the power of search engines to your benefit.

pay and display

The major search engines have always denied that you can reach the top of search engine lists by opening your cheque-book. However, many businesses have benefited by paying for banner ads whenever someone types in relevant keywords. The Californian dentist Harold Ganz, who specialises in halitosis, pays AOL and Yahoo! over $50,000 a year. For this, his banner ad appears every time the keywords 'bad breath', 'halitosis' or 'fresh breath' are typed in to the search engine. One major European search engine, Godado, has controversially taken this one stage further by charging businesses to register on the search engine and displaying how much they pay for all to see.

Whether or not such a cynical approach will work, however, remains to be seen. In general, search engine users (for obvious reasons) prefer engines that rank sites on the basis of their quality.

concentrate on quality

Increasingly, search engines are employing panels of experts to rank sites on the basis of their quality. At Lycos, for instance, a team of human experts is responsible for choosing the first ten results in a search. The next three results are determined by the popularity of sites and the remainder are based on keywords embedded in a site as found by Lycos' robot.

Search engines exist to provide a worthwhile service to people searching at their sites. It therefore doesn't matter how many tricks you use to get your site ranked in a preferential position; if it doesn't make the grade you have little chance of being indexed.

refresh your site

As people are more likely to come back to a site that is updated, search engines rank regularly refreshed sites higher than those with unchanging content. Furthermore, links that lead to an out-of-date address can easily be checked by search engines, so make sure your links work.

obtain your own domain name

Domain name registration provides one easy way for search engines to discriminate among the plethora of sites submitted to them. Thus, 'www.mysite.com' would be given preference over 'www.demon.net/mysite'.

evaluate your success

To see how successful your efforts have been, you can use a free online tool called Rank This (www.rankthis.com), which shows where your site is positioned on all the main search engines when people type in your keywords. You should monitor your ranking at least once a month – positions can change at breakneck speed as new sites are submitted and old ones updated.

There are many software products available that monitor how people arrive at your site. They not only tell you whether or not they used a search engine, but also which search engine they used and what keywords they typed in. Visit Search Engine Watch (at www.searchenginewatch.com) for more information.

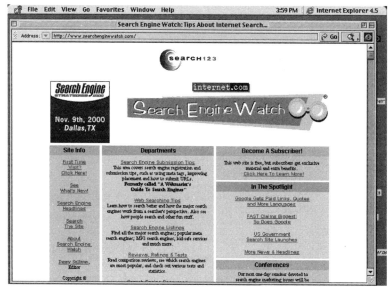

Figure 6.2 *The Search Engine Watch site provides a mine of information on all the leading search engines*

the seven deadly search engine sins

Many companies still believe that the best way to arrive at the top of the search engine lists is to cheat. While in the early days of the Web it was possible to get away with sneaky tactics, now the search engines have all wised up. If you are caught in the act, you are likely to be blacklisted, not only from that particular engine but from all the major search sites and directories. The following methods should therefore be resisted at all costs:

- *Using inappropriate keywords* Keyword combinations such as 'hot sex action' and 'free money' may get people to your site, but you need to remember that when it comes to site traffic, quality, not quantity, is what is important.
- *Using the same keyword more than once* Adding the same keyword more than once in your META tags used to be accepted practice. Now, 'keyword stuffing' is frowned on and the search engine robots trawling the Web looking for sites will deliberately ignore stacked keywords. However, it is perfectly acceptable to put different synonyms or related words in META tags, such as 'PR, public relations, marketing, promotion, publicity'.
- *Stealing META tags* Copying another site's META tag structure is illegal and probably the most severe search engine sin of all. Many Web site owners have ended up in court as a result of META tag plagiarism.
- *Submitting different pages of the same file* If a site has more than one page, it is not automatically expected to have more than one submission.
- *Using multiple titles* Search engines will only acknowledge one META tag title per page.
- *Putting competitors' names into META tags* While it may seem logical to incorporate the names of competitors within a META tag (to catch visitors typing their names into a search engine), it is a breach of copyright. For a while, it was unclear whether or not it was acceptable to use the trademarks of other businesses as META tags because no case had come to court. However, recently there have been several cases on both sides of the Atlantic centred solely on the issue of

META tags. For instance, the UK-based company Roadtech sued another company for trademark infringement and 'passing off', having taken Roadtech customers away by using META tags. Roadtech was awarded £15,000 in damages.

▧ *Submitting different URLs of the same site* Sites with more than one URL or Web site address may be tempted to pretend they are two separate sites. As soon as the search engine robot sees the identical HTML script, though, it will reject the submission.

While all of these techniques can work in theory, in practice the risks are too high. Ultimately, the best chance of being indexed on a search engine is to have a site that is a hit with its target audience.

be patient

Although the Internet is typically viewed as a fast-moving medium, search engine registration is a notoriously slow process. It often takes over a month and several attempts before the engine will list your site. However, if at first you don't succeed, you really must dust yourself off and try again. It can take as many as ten submission attempts before someone at Yahoo! will have a look at it. If, after all this, you are still not getting anywhere, you may have to rejig your META tags, page titles and even content then resubmit your site. It takes time, but will eventually pay off.

In cyberspace, the old cliché still holds true: all good things come to those who wait. The reason so many good sites remain unlisted is because they give up on search engines halfway through. If you have faith in your site, you shouldn't give up on it until you see it in the top ten sites in the categories you want to be listed under.

summary

Search engines are the main way people find where they are going online. If your site is not included on any of the most popular search engines, it is, quite simply, off the map.

Not only is search engine registration essential, you also need to ensure your site ranks highly when a user types relevant keywords. Very few people will be prepared to visit your site if it is ranked fortieth in the search results.

To achieve a high ranking, you need to take time over your META tags and think carefully when you are filling in search site submission forms. You also need to be prepared to rework your strategy if you fail first time round.

Once your site has been included, you need to think of other ways to direct traffic towards your site. These will be explained in the next chapter.

promoting your site

Although the old maxim 'the best things in life are free' rarely proves true in the business world, when it comes to Internet marketing it really does, for while there are numerous ways in which you can spend money on promoting your site online, the most effective methods generally cost nothing at all. This is because the Internet's democratic nature means that word of mouth and unbiased recommendations count a lot more than advertising and sponsorship deals. So, before you start letting the word out, you need to be completely confident that your site is more than a one-click wonder. If it is unlikely to attract repeat traffic, then, no matter how comprehensive your marketing efforts are, they are likely to prove ineffective.

Although registering with the major search engines is the most obvious way to start your marketing campaign, it is only the beginning. Outlined below are some of the other cost-effective ways to publicise your site.

seek reciprocal links

Once you have registered your site with the main search engines, your next step should be to seek links with other sites.

Search for related sites that attract a similar target audience, then e-mail the relevant Webmasters.

The sites that are listed near yours on search engines would be the most obvious ones to approach in the first instance (provided that they are not immediate competitors). The easiest sites to gain reciprocal links with tend to be information only ones, as they have no rival products to sell.

When e-mailing the Webmaster concerned, make sure your message is as specific as possible by mentioning their site and how much you like it (flattery will get you everywhere on the Internet). Tell them that you have an interest in a similar audience. Ask them for a link and tell them also what you would be willing to do for them at your site. If the site you are approaching sells products, you could also offer to give some of them a plug, providing of course that they are not products you already sell. Remember that when Webmasters read the message they will be asking themselves 'What's in it for me?' As with so many other areas of e-business, the more you are willing to give, the more you are likely to receive in return.

contact the online media

As the Internet is a fast-moving, ever-evolving medium, there are always sites out there hungry for new information. Contacting editors of e-zines, online journals and newsletters about your site can therefore prove very worthwhile. To find relevant sites, you should take a look at the major search engines. Yahoo! has a comprehensive index of all the e-media directories at the following address:

www.yahoo.com/News_and_Media/Web_Directories

Another great resource for e-media is the New Jour site (http://gort.ucsd.edu/newjour/). As well as listing new and archived e-zines and journals, it also provides a wide-ranging index of electronic newsletters, most of which are not listed elsewhere. A user-friendly search engine at the site allows visitors to search by either category or keyword.

Sites such as Media UK (www.mediauk.com) incorporate e-mail addresses along with other contact information. The Journalist's Notepad (www.tech.prsa.org/journal.html) is another excellent source of relevant e-mail addresses for international e-media.

The following guidelines should be taken into account when making initial contact with e-zines and other e-media:

- *Think beyond press releases* When contacting site editors, try to think beyond the standard press release format.

- *Target each contact individually* Don't contact different editors with the same message – make sure each editor receives a tailored message.

Figure 7.1 *The Media UK homepage*

▨ *Offer something in return*   One of the easiest ways to gain publicity is to offer it to someone else. You could provide a link to the target site or mention their publication in your newsletter.

▨ *Contribute articles*   If you can write pretty well, it may be worthwhile offering to contribute an article. When you do this, make sure your site or business receives a mention at the foot of the piece.

▨ *Avoid 'snooze news'*   Launching or upgrading your site does not amount in itself to a good news story. Instead, you need to think in terms of how your site helps the people visiting it and find a way of demonstrating the unique qualities of your site.

▨ *Be topical*   When contacting editors about your site, try to put a topical spin on the information you present.

contribute to newsgroups

Once your site is up and running, one of the best things you can do to get free publicity is to contribute to 'Usenet' newsgroups. These groups are, in effect, online communities, grouped together because of a mutual interest rather than geographical situation. The tens of thousands of newsgroups cover every topic imaginable, from accountancy to zoology, so you are more than likely to find at least one group relevant to your business.

To search all the newsgroups collected under Usenet, visit Deja (www.dejanews.com), which has the most comprehensive newsgroups search engine available. Then, when you have typed in appropriate keywords to find groups relevant to your business, follow the steps outlined below:

▨ *Lurk*   Before you post a message to a group, you

should become a mute visitor for a while. 'Lurk' around and get a feel for the discussion and the dynamics of the group. Look at what sort of messages incite the best responses. The reason this is so important is because discussion groups are used by the most Net-literate members of the online population. As such, they are well versed in the rules of online etiquette (or netiquette as it's known). Anyone leaving inappropriate messages or writing with an explicit commercial interest will be 'flamed' down with a barrage of negative responses.

▧ *Create a 'signature line'* A signature line is a sentence or two at the end of your message that gives a flavour of your business or your site. This is the only area of your message where you can get away with blatant promotion. Make sure you include your e-mail and site address.

▧ *Advise, don't advertise* Members of newsgroups want information, not advertising. Keep messages relevant to the subject topic and, when responding to questions relevant to your business area, quote from the message you are responding to. Always remember to write as a real person rather than as a sales rep. While offering advice, also ask questions to engage people in ongoing discussion.

▧ *Answer questions* The easiest way to gain credibility in newsgroups is to provide useful answers to questions.

▧ *Keep messages brief* Try to make sure messages run to fewer than 200 words.

advertising

While the jury is still out on banner advertising, the case for the defence is gaining ground. An Andersen Consulting survey of around 1,500 Internet users discovered that banners are generally more effective than TV or radio ads in luring Web shoppers. According to the survey, banner ads drove 25 per cent of users to shop online, beating newspaper or magazine ads (which only brought in 14 per cent). However, to paraphrase the Victorian Prime Minister Benjamin Disraeli, there are three kinds of e-business lies: lies, damned lies and survey findings.

The fact remains that, by and large, Internet users remain cynical regarding online advertising and are reluctant to click-through a banner to the advertiser's site.

Online advertising is not going to bring immediate sales. It is only really effective in the long term, in building brands online. However, to build a brand via advertising takes considerable amounts of money and this is only really an option for the e-business big guns. My advice is to sell advertising space on your own site before you pay for it on someone else's. Also, if you are adamant that advertising is the way forward, test the water first by signing up to a banner exchange programme (see below).

banner exchange programmes

If you want to try out online advertising for free, your best bet is to join one of the many banner exchange programmes. Once you have designed a banner that promotes your site, all you need to do is submit it to the programme and offer to put ads for other people's sites on yours. The banner exchange site sends you different banners and records how many times banners are displayed. This record is then used to monitor your credits. Your banner ad is sent to other sites according to how many credits you have gathered. Some services even provide free credits when you sign up, which means that your banner can be displayed on other sites straight away.

Although banner programmes are not going to bring in phenomenal amounts of site traffic, if you are prepared to place banners on your own site, they may be worth a try. The main problem with them, however, is that they provide you with a very restricted choice as to where and when your banner appears.

For more information on banner exchanges check out the following sites:

- 1-2-3 Free Banner Exchange at www.1-2-free.com
- BannerSwap at www.bannerswap.com
- LinkExchange at www.linkexchange.com
- UK Banners at www.ukbanners.com

Figure 7.2 *UK Banners is the leading banner exchange site in the UK*

Web rings

Web rings are linked communities of related sites. Every site taking part in the ring will link to the previous and next site in the ring as well as to a main page, giving a comprehensive list of all the sites taking part. The name comes from the fact that all the sites in the ring are linked together in a virtual circle, so, if users carry on clicking the next link continuously, they will return to the site from where they started.

The largest organiser of Web rings at the time of writing is WebRing (dir.webring.yahoo.com). WebRing coordinates around 50,000 rings with over half a million sites taking part in them. At their site, you can trawl through the vast array of different rings on offer to see if any are suitable for you.

The great thing about Web rings compared to banner exchanges is that they allow you to target your audience with much greater precision. By joining a Web ring that is related to the content of your own site, you will tap into the audiences of similar sites.

For further information on Web rings, visit the following Yahoo! page:

dir.yahoo.com/computers_and_internet/internet/world_wide_
web/searching_the_web/indices_to_web_documents/rings/

promoting at your site

There are various ways in which you can encourage people to return to your site while they are visiting it. These include the following.

bookmarking

Placing a notice at your site saying 'Bookmark this site' may not seem the most subtle approach, but it can be surprisingly effective. You could also encourage people to add your site to their 'Favorites' menu.

e-mail newsletters

One of the best ways to keep your business and its Web site firmly in the minds of customers is to send out an online newsletter. By providing informative articles of interest to your customers, you can boost your reputation as an authority on your specialist areas. Furthermore, if you incorporate a link to your site in a newsletter, you are likely to generate repeat visits.

Setting up a newsletter involves devoting a Web page to it. You need to ensure that readers have reasons to subscribe and then tell them how to do so by including something similar to the following statement:

> To subscribe to our weekly/monthly/bi-monthly newsletter, send an e-mail to newsletter@mycompany.com with the word 'subscribe' in the subject line.

That's the easy part. The hard bit is coming up with the relevant content. You want to make sure that the newsletter is appropriate to your business without giving subscribers the hard sell. If you are in the service sector, the newsletter could follow a guide format. A solicitors firm, for instance, could provide a legal advice guide. If you sell products, you need to think about what interests your target audience. If you sell world music CDs, for example, you might decide to include features on relevant artists and events and to supplement them with occasional reviews of new additions to your stock list.

The size and frequency of your newsletter is not that important. The main thing is that you don't overburden either yourself or your subscribers by offering too much information too often. I personally find that sending out a 1,000-word newsletter monthly strikes the right balance between feeling too pressured and forgetting about it.

Here are some guidelines for creating successful newsletters:

- *Make your newsletter useful* Think of the information your customers want rather than the message you want to get across. People will drop out of your e-mailing lists if your newsletter is, in effect, glorified spam. To make your newsletter objective, get relevant journalists involved or ask for suggestions from subscribers via e-mail.
- *Don't make it too long* If your newsletter is too long, it is likely to be deleted before it is read.
- *Send it out regularly* Once you have decided on the frequency of your newsletter, you need to stick to it.
- *Collect e-mail addresses from your site* To collect e-mail addresses from your site, you need to set up a subscription form that links to your own e-mail system. Web-building software, such as Dreamweaver or Microsoft Front Page, will be able to do this for you. Make it clear that any information people give you will remain confidential and not be sold on to mailing-list companies.
- *Use links* Make good use of Web links in your newsletter. Some newsletters are simply a collection of fantastic links centred on an appropriate theme.

Also, when laying out your newsletter, there are some basic rules to follow to make its presentation in a subscribers' browser more effective:

- put line spaces between paragraphs to break up the text and make it easy to read;
- don't centre your text – your newsletter will appear differently on different e-mail programs, so don't try to centre or justify your text as it may look drastically different on someone else's computer screen;
- avoid using monospace fonts, such as Ariel and

Courier, where every letter takes up the same amount of space as they look entirely different on each e-mail software program;

▩ remember to spellcheck your newsletter;

▩ send the newsletter to yourself or a friend or colleague before you send it out to check that it looks all right;

▩ when sending out your e-mail newsletter, remember to use the Bcc: line to conceal the recipient's e-mail addresses from each other.

'e-mail this to a friend' notices

Putting an 'e-mail this to a friend' button at the foot of popular articles or pictures is a good way of encouraging 'word of Web' publicity.

online events

If you have a live chat facility at your site, you can encourage people to return to take part in a forthcoming online 'e-vent'. This could be in the form of a seminar, question-and-answer session or other activity that will enable you to show off your expertise.

announce site updates

As well as mentioning site updates in newsletters and other e-mailouts, you should make it clear at your site which sections are updated and how often.

set up an e-mailing list

If you want to make sure you stay in touch with your customers, you should set up your own e-mailing list. This can be used to send out newsletters, site update announcements, and information on new products, and will help you to conduct consumer research. Such postings will not only remind your customers that you still exist, but also, especially if you include a link to your site, serve to encourage repeat traffic.

To set up your own list, you will need to use list-serving software, which manages mailing lists automatically. Fortunately, most of this software can be downloaded for free. The two main products are Listserve (www.listserve.com) and Majordomo (www.majordomo.com).

promoting your site in the real world

Your online marketing efforts need to be supplemented and supported by offline marketing if your site is to make the maximum impact. After all, your online customers live in the real world, not cyberspace.

Here are some of the possibilities for expanding your marketing efforts beyond the realms of the Internet:

contact the offline media

The offline media are fascinated by juicy Internet stories. If you can come up with one about your Web site that puts an imaginative slant on it and relates to the 'bricks and mortar' world, you are sure to gain media coverage. Most newspapers have Internet or technology-based sections or supplements and there are many TV and radio shows with Net features. There is also a rapidly expanding range of Internet magazines that you can target. Many include a 'site of the month' or similar feature, alongside various other references to new or improved Web sites. If, by commissioning or conducting research, you can shed some light on the ways in which people like to use the Net or how online habits are evolving, you will have an advantage over your purely Web-based competition. Companies that are first to do something online also stand a good chance of gaining press interest.

put your Web address everywhere

When your Web site is up and running, your URL (Web site address) needs maximum exposure. The aim is for people to become as familiar (if not more so) with your site address as they are with the name of your company. Anything you produce to promote your business should include your URL – business cards, letterheads, signs, pens, adverts, brochures and so on.

When you have the space, you should also make people aware of what the main reason is for coming to your site. One of the easiest ways to do this is to pose a question and then say 'find the answer at www.yoursite.com.' This is a tactic the Royal Mail has used to great effect to promote its Web site. It asks a question, such as 'How can you cut your business over-heads by 40 per cent?', then follows it with 'Find out at www.royalmail.com.' This works because it arouses interest and clearly defines a target audience simultaneously.

use direct marketing methods

While direct marketing and, in particular, 'spam' (or junk e-mail) is no longer effective or acceptable on the Internet, it can still be worthwhile offline. However, sending out mail shots will only work if the content of your site is directly relevant to the people on your mailing list. Make sure your letters are as tailored and personal as possible.

advertise offline

Advertising in the real world can prove more effective than

advertising online, but it is often more expensive. If you are investing substantial sums of money in an offline advertising campaign, it is important to remain realistic. According to one US report in autumn 2000, despite high levels of TV advertising for Web sites, 25 per cent of adults couldn't name one site (remember that American Internet usage is generally considered to be two years ahead of that in the UK).

events

The Internet can be used as a hook to involve people at your stand in an exhibition. You can show people your site, ask them to subscribe to your e-newsletter and even distribute CD ROMs for your site and other e-material. There are also numerous high-profile Internet exhibitions and conferences that could provide you with valuable networking opportunities. The search engines for AltaVista, Yahoo! and Lycos are especially helpful for finding out about relevant Internet and trade exhibitions.

summary

Although many businesses spend over 70 per cent of their Internet budget on marketing their site, many of the most effective promotional methods cost nothing at all. Furthermore, word of mouth travels a lot faster on the Net than it does offline, so, providing your site is satisfying its audience, your users may end up promoting your site on your behalf. In fact, a lot of the most effective marketing successes, such as AltaVista and Microsoft's Hotmail service, became famous before any money was spent on advertising. When your site catches the imagination of its audience, as these examples prove, the results can be priceless.

building your
e-brand

On the Internet, your competition is always only a few clicks away. To make sure your visitors keep coming back to you rather than your rivals, you need to create an easily identifiable brand. Depending on the quality of your products or services is not enough, you need to think of ways in which you can add value to your customer's online experience.

brand power

A brand and a product (or service) are two entirely separate things. This point can be illustrated with an offline example. When the head of Coca-Cola, Robert Goizuenta, became aware of the fact that Pepsi beat Coca-Cola in taste tests, he decided to come up with a new and improved formula to trial across America. The drink – called New Coke – was launched in the United States and Coca-Cola instantly started to lose money. People preferred the original product because they had grown loyal to the brand. They didn't care if the new product tasted better, they wanted the original Coke back. Within a year, the old brand was reinstated.

This proves that, in the real world, brand power wins over product power every time.

On the Internet, branding is equally important, although it works in a different way. While Coca-Cola took years to build up its brand, on the Internet things move a lot quicker. As the head of the US division of Saatchi & Saatchi, Kevin Roberts, tells us, 'On the Internet your business can become a legendary, mythical thing in six months.'

The Internet is the perfect brand-building tool because it enables customers to communicate with businesses at a deeper level than ever before. Instead of sitting passively in front of a 30-second TV advertisement, customers can interact for 15 minutes or so with the company at their Web site.

information and interactivity

When deciding how to brand your e-business, it is essential to keep in mind the essential features of the Internet: information and interactivity. These characteristics provide both new opportunities and threats for brand building.

On the downside, these aspects mean that you cannot take as much control over your brand message as you can offline. Anyone with a grievance against your company can voice that grievance in front of thousands of other people. This is a lesson that many high-profile brands have had to learn the hard way. The plethora of anti-sites – from Microsucks.com to British Scareways (www.aviation-uk.com) – testify to this phenomenon. However, if you welcome and respond to consumer feedback at your site, this downside can largely be avoided.

Furthermore, if your Web site encourages contributions from its online audience, your brand's message becomes more closely aligned to consumer opinion than ever before. This leads us to a new Web watchword: personalisation.

personalisation

The principles behind branding online are, in many ways, diametrically opposed to branding offline.

In the real world, the aim of branding is often to create a singular, unified, monolithic identity. Thus, a single message is usually used to communicate to as many people as possible. Successful slogans that originate in the real world are therefore often non-specific, catch-all statements – 'Just do it', 'The real thing' and so on. The reason for this is that the offline marketing methods are passive: TV adverts, direct mail shots, billboards and the other tools of promoting a brand in the real world deny interactivity. The result is that the people viewing the brand message have no say over the content of that message.

On the Internet, however, people pull information (and the 'brand message') towards them. This means that, in this environment, brands do the opposite of what they do in the real world: they become personalised because information is tailored to and by the end user. You can have 'My Yahoo!', 'My Excite' and 'My MSN'. In fact, any site with more than, say, three pages provides personalised content for its users, as it gives them a choice of information.

The best way to personalise your site is to enable visitors to contribute to the content itself. This helps you to bring consumers closer to your brand than ever before. Outlined below are some of the ways in which you can increase the 'click factor' by adding high interactivity to your site.

set up an online forum

Web-based forums and message boards are excellent means of introducing interactivity at your site as they enable visitors to contribute in no small way to the site's content. They also mean that people can talk to each other about issues relating to your site and therefore provide a form of 'dot community', making people feel as if they belong to your site. This sense of belonging is the most valuable aspect of online branding, as it strengthens consumer solidarity with your site and what it has to offer. Message boards also show, in the most explicit way possible, that you as a company are more than willing to listen to what your customers have to say.

Before setting up an online forum up at your site, try a few out at other sites. They come in various different formats. The most effective forums and message boards enable you to follow the thread of conversations, retaining a self-explanatory structure that is ordered by chronology or subject.

Two of the most popular forum software products are O'Reilly WebBoard (www.webboard.oreilly.com) and WWWBoard (available at www.worldwidemart.com/scripts). These can both be downloaded free of charge.

For more general information on forums and messages boards visit the Guide2Web site (www.guide2web.com).

add a guestbook

One of the most effective ways of encouraging interactivity is to add a guestbook to your site. Guestbooks are of particular use for sites with a small but geographically diverse customer base. Visitors can write their comments about your site to share with you and other visitors. A word of warning, however: if you provide a forum for people to comment about your site, you should not be surprised if some of the comments are irrelevant, negative or insulting. This is the drawback of encouraging feedback, but if you keep an open mind, criticism can prove more constructive than flattery.

Dreambook (www.dreambook.com) offers an effective guestbook program that can be tailored to fit in with the rest of your pages. With this system, banner ads will be displayed on your guestbook unless you pay to remove them. FreeCode (www.freecode.com) also offers a range of free packages that you can put on your Web server.

include a search engine

If your site increases beyond 30 or so text-based pages, you might decide to add a search engine. This can be a great way to enhance one-to-one relationships with your visitors, as it allows them to customise your site to their own requirements. It is also the ultimate navigation aid, helping visitors to find things of interest to them as quickly as possible.

One of the best search software products on the market is Atomz (www.atomz.com) and it is free. The program presents search results in an easily adapted page so you can adjust the HTML code to make it look like one of your own Web pages.

run a chat room

Chat rooms combine interaction with up-to-the-minute immediacy to impressive effect. Furthermore, although it involves quite complicated technical programming, chat software can be downloaded for free at The Free Site (www.thefreesite.com) and at Hypermart (www.hypermart.net). Before downloading chat software, make sure you check how many people can chat live together.

Although chat rooms are great for sites seeking a 'fun' brand identity, they are not generally suited for corporate-minded or business-to-business sites. Also, if you are going to run a chat room, make sure your site attracts enough traffic to make it a valid enterprise. After all, it's better to have no chat room than it is to have an empty one.

think fast and fresh

Successful branding online depends on your ability to keep up with the frenetic pace of Internet time. It also depends on establishing long-term site–visitor relations. To do both of these things, you will need to regularly update the site's content. To maintain a fresh and fast-moving site, try doing the following:

- ▦ *Plan ahead* When planning your site, you should decide which pages you are going to update and how often.
- ▦ *Update small sections regularly* If you have the time and resources, you should update very small sections daily (such as a 'Tip of the Day'), then slightly longer sections on a weekly basis.
- ▦ *Never let information become out of date* Information that is clearly out of date will devalue and undermine your online brand.
- ▦ *Add a newsfeed* If you want to make sure your site has an up-to-date relevance without spending too much time, you could add a newsfeed to your site. Moreover (www.moreover.com) provides a general newsfeed free to Web sites. Simply sign up at the Moreover site, then cut and paste a chunk of HTML to insert into your own site. Tailored, subject-oriented newsfeeds are available from Screaming Media (www.screamingmedia.com), although, unfortunately, you have to pay for them.

be imaginative

If your site is intended to support your offline efforts, you will have to think long and hard about what will bring traffic to your site. It isn't enough to assume that there are thousands of Internet users out there just dying to learn more about your brand and its values – some lateral thinking is needed.

Imagine that you are selling washing powder in the real world. 'It's going to be hard', you might be thinking, 'to bring traffic to my site.' Persil (www.persil.com), however, overcame this by coming up with the imaginative idea of a 'Stain removal' section, providing advice on how to get rid of different kinds of stains on fabrics. This is something virtually everyone is likely to need at some time and clearly fits with the Persil product range. So, be imaginative and think of what people will find really useful.

Figure 8.1   *Persil's Web site is an example of an imaginative support site that is of real value to its users*

think laterally

If you sell a product or service online, you may need to do some lateral thinking in order to make a strong impact. After all, it is very unlikely – no matter how specific your particular product or service is – that there is no one else offering something similar somewhere else.

Of course, in the real world this isn't a problem. If you sell pet products in Southampton, say, you don't really feel threatened by Pete's Pet Store in Sydney. On the Internet, however, all your competitors are only a few clicks away. The absence of geography means you cannot rely on the quality of your goods alone. You need, instead, to think of who you are targeting and what else they would be interested in.

Think of the two key characteristics of the Internet mentioned earlier: interactivity and information. If you are the Southampton-based pet products site, for instance, you could provide information in the form of a 'Pets' Diets' page, providing advice on how to give your pets a balanced diet. You could even get the assistance of a vet and provide animal health advice. You could then make this information interactive by putting it in a question and answer format, whereby visitors to the site can e-mail questions relating to their pets.

exclusive information

As the Internet is all about information, one way to make sure you attract repeat traffic is to provide relevant and exclusive information. By providing unique and useful material that is unavailable anywhere else on the Web, you will be virtually guaranteed a steady stream of visitors. If you sell theatre tickets, for instance, you could provide exclusive reviews from West End premieres or forthcoming productions.

incorporate feedback

When it comes to marketing, brands can be developed or damaged in a very short space of time. The key to success or failure depends on the two-way architecture of the Web. While brand builders who acknowledge and encourage the Net's feedback culture are going to be able to create a successful brand, those who deny and ignore negative 'word of Web' comments are going to be in trouble.

'On the Internet, markets are getting more connected and more powerfully vocal every day', says David Weinberger, co-author of the highly influential *Cluetrain Manifesto*. 'Every product you can name, from fashion to office supplies, can be discussed, argued over, researched and bought as part of a vast conversation among the people interested in it.' The powerful e-brands are the ones that engage and move with this conversation. Take Amazon (.com or .co.uk). Its visitors post their opinions on books they have read and read the opinions of other visitors before deciding whether or not to make a purchase.

Brands only become vulnerable on the Internet if consumers are denied access to their development. If, however, conversation between the brand and its market is positively encouraged via bulletin boards, e-mail correspondence, e-surveys and so on, the Internet is actually an advantage. Brands can develop faster, mistakes can be rectified more quickly and the brand message itself evolves into a mutually beneficial conversation.

learning from successful e-brands

One of the most effective ways in which you can start thinking imaginatively about your e-brand is to look at other sites that have created a strong sense of identity.

Amazon – perhaps the most famous online brand of all – built its reputation on one concept: simplicity. Its hassle-free one-click shopping system has become the stuff of Internet legend, which is why Amazon has warned off imitators by patenting the process.

Yahoo!, the other leading e-brand, works by understanding its purpose. When Jerry Yang set it up back in 1994, he realised Yahoo! was a place 'people visit to go somewhere else'. His aim was therefore the exact opposite of the normal e-branding aim: he wanted to help people leave his site as quickly as possible. To this day, the Yahoo! site – with its speedy search process and straightforward homepage – remains true to this original intention.

However, it is not just businesses that originated online that can create successful e-brands. The following examples show how four very different companies have strengthened their brands online.

Hot Hot Hot (www.hothothot.com)

Hot Hot Hot.com, has exploited its niche as an e-tailer selling hot sauce.

The site has never spent any money on advertising. Instead, it relies on word of mouth. With a tight rein on marketing and other costs, the site manages to make a substantial profit. As Hot Hot Hot's Ben Arora says, 'we don't want to fall into the same trap as the dot.coms who are spending more than they can ever earn.'

Hot Hot Hot continues to compete in its now crowded niche. It is doing this by moving into the business-to-business market (other distributors, e-stores and restaurants) as well as by making sure its sauces remain the hottest. The business-to-business sector now accounts for 60 per cent of the company's total revenue.

easyJet (www.easyjet.com)

In April 1998, easyJet started offering online reservations, and the site quickly became a central part of its business. In November 1999, the company sold over half of its seats online for the first time; by September 2000 it was regularly selling 70 per cent of its 120,000 weekly tickets on the Web.

There are a number of reasons for this rapid shift to cyber-space. First, the airline offers small but significant discounts to people who book over the Internet. EasyJet has also taken the risky measure of making it more difficult to place phone reservations. Since May 2000, customers have been required to use

Figure 8.2 *Hot Hot Hot remains at the top in a now crowded niche market*

the site for bookings more than two months in advance. They have realised that online bookings cost them a lot less than those taken in a call centre. Their online bookings are now ticketed electronically, too, with an e-mail confirmation.

Sainsbury's: Taste for Life (www.tasteforlife.co.uk)

Taste for Life is a site intended to support the brand identity of Sainsbury's, the UK-based supermarket chain. Instead of bombarding visitors with the Sainsbury's logo and product range, however, it takes a significantly more customer-focused approach to 'brand interaction'.

The site concentrates on providing visitors with useful relevant food and drink information and features one of the largest recipe search engines on the Web. It allows visitors to customise the information they receive to such an extent that they can search out recipes based on different criteria, such as nationality, cooking time, ingredients and health requirements.

Significantly, the ingredients listed in recipes aren't based solely on Sainsbury's items. This lends the site more authority and, subsequently, more brand loyalty.

Procter & Gamble: Physique (www.physique.com)

Procter & Gamble is another company that is starting to come round to the virtues of cyber branding. It has decided to launch its newest haircare product, 'Physique', with a Web-intensive campaign. Having spent a phenomenal 70 per cent of its promotional budget on the Internet, Physique has already become Procter & Gamble's most visited site.

The central idea behind the site is the Physique club – an online community that provides Procter & Gamble with valuable feedback, while at the same time ensuring a strong core of loyal customers. The online brand becomes synonymous with the community and therefore evolves with it. As a result, the issue of finding out what the customer wants becomes largely irrelevant because, in such an instance, the brand is the customer.

summary

To differentiate your Web site from the competition, you need to take e-branding very seriously. By thinking of ways to personalise the online experience and tailoring content to meet users' requirements, you will be able to strengthen relations between your business and its customers.

As many successful e-brands have shown, imagination and lateral thinking go a long way in cyberspace.

the Internet inside your business

The significance of the Internet as a business tool extends far beyond marketing and sales. Perhaps the most important way in which the Internet can affect business is from the inside. While the rest of this book looks at how the Internet can improve your business standing in the outside world, this chapter looks at how it can revolutionise your business from within.

e-mail

As e-mail is arguably the most convenient communications tool of all, it has immense benefits for internal relationships. It can be used for brainstorming and decision making as well as a means of increasing communication between different departments, such as marketing and accounts.

As Adam Joinson, a psychologist at the Open University, points out, 'If someone puts you on the spot by asking you a question, you may answer rashly. But using e-mail gives you the time to craft a sensible, articulate response.'

It's also a great memory aid. Instead of reminding people one by one of a meeting weeks ago, you can send a single e-mail message.

Other reasons for e-mail being such an effective means of internal communication include:

- ▓ *feedback* e-mail enables the free flow of ideas within an organisation as it is easy to click and respond to messages;
- ▓ *contacting field staff* because the Internet can be accessed anywhere with the help of laptops and wireless application protocol (WAP or 'third generation') mobile phones, e-mail can keep you in touch with your field staff anywhere in the country or around the globe;
- ▓ *cost* you can communicate with colleagues or employees around the world for a minimal cost;
- ▓ *functionality* reports, spreadsheets, proposals, reminders and other documents can be sent via e-mail, either as attachments or embedded in the main text;
- ▓ *maximum disclosure* in a study conducted by Oxford University into different methods of communication, it emerged that people using e-mail disclosed four times as much as those communicating face to face or via a video-conferencing camera, and, as Adam Joinson maintains, 'when using e-mail we can concentrate on the message, not the way we present it';
- ▓ *equality* differences relating to race, gender and disability are rendered irrelevant in e-mail messages.

developing an e-mail policy

For all its virtues, however, e-mail use must be organised and regulated within your business. As e-mail is often seen as an informal method of communication, people often lower their guard when sending electronic messages. This can result in messages that are inappropriate or, at worst, illegal. By providing an e-mail policy, you can give your staff a code of practice within which they can work. Such a policy should be designed to encourage effective communication and should therefore resist being too restrictive. A successful e-mail policy should:

- specify when e-mail should be used in place of other communication methods (and when it shouldn't);
- encourage employees to organise e-mails into folders;
- state what kinds of messages are allowed to be sent;
- highlight the risks of opening attached files (due to viruses).

There should also be a limit to the number of times people check their messages during the course of an average working day, so they're not being constantly interrupted.

e-mail netiquette

As well as highlighting the above risks, an e-mail policy should also tell employees how to capitalise on the benefits of e-mail. To do this, there will need to be guidelines on e-mail etiquette (or netiquette). This should include the following 10 points:

- be friendly and polite in all correspondence;
- where possible, avoid sending attached files;
- write in plain English – as e-mail is an informal medium, avoid business jargon and being too formal;
- only use HTML-formatted files when you know the person you are sending to has a software program that can read them;
- keep messages brief – in most cases, messages should be under 20 lines long;

■ respond quickly to messages, especially if they are sent by customers;

■ only send messages to people who need to receive them – do not over use the Cc: (carbon copy) and Bcc: (blind carbon copy) facilities;

■ check spelling, grammar and readability;

■ make sure the subject line is clear, succinct and relevant;

■ every e-mail message should have a definite purpose.

You should also make sure people realise that clogging up the system with irrelevant messages, such as jokes or chain e-mail, inhibits effective business communication.

e-newsletters within your business

If you have quite a large workforce, electronic newsletters are a good way of using the Internet to build a sense of community among your staff. They can be used to announce company and staff news, new appointments, upcoming training courses, staff events, promotions and any vacancies open to present staff.

The benefit of the internal e-newsletter over its offline counterpart is that it can be used to encourage greater interactivity. The Internet enables people to provide feedback on anything they want to respond to in the newsletter. To generate interest in your newsletter, you could ask employees or colleagues to contribute feature articles or make other content suggestions.

internal e-mailing lists

To use e-mail to communicate effectively with employees, it may be useful to compile an e mailing list of every member of staff.

Once you have put the full list together, you should then divide it into subcategories relating to different departments – marketing, accounts, human resources, sales and so on. This will enable you to limit the number of messages sent by ensuring that only those people who need to read them get them. When you do need to send everyone in your company the same e-mail message, you will also have all their addresses ready prepared.

Web sites and your staff

Having a good Web site will provide your staff with something solid for them to identify themselves with, as well as showing any potential new employees what an exciting business you are to work for. According to one recent survey, over 70 per cent of graduates claimed that the quality of prospective employers' Web sites influences their decision as to whether or not to apply.

Here are some of the ways in which your Web site can be used to improve internal relationships:

▓ *Include staff on your site* Many businesses add the personal touch to their Web sites by having a 'Staff' or 'People' section. If you have a relatively small firm, you might be able to include every member of staff on the site at once. If, on the other hand, you are a large business, you could have different members of staff appear every time the site is updated. Asda (www.asda.com) includes members of its shop staff on the site in the role of 'site guides', assisting users as they travel their way around each of the product sections. Many other sites draw on staff expertise by getting them involved in 'Q&A' or 'Ask the expert'-type features.

■ *Involve staff when building your site* To make sure your site is truly representative of your business, you should involve as many members of staff in the design process as possible. By asking employees what they think should be incorporated on the site, you will not only be making them feel valued, but you could also end up with a better-quality site as a direct result.

■ *Have a 'staff news' section* By including a staff news page, you will be able to maintain staff interest in your site and involve staff in its content.

intranets

Intranets are mini-Internets that only allow access to people within your organisation. The technology they use is identical to that of the Internet – the difference is that it only works within the limits of a private, localised network. They are referred to as local area networks (LANs).

Intranets, like the Internet, enable users to set up Web sites as well as to send and receive e-mail messages. They allow people to access information within an organisation, while prohibiting external users from doing so. Furthermore, employers can use the same e-mail program to exchange messages both with other intranet users and the Internet.

Intranets have the following advantages:

■ *Security* Intranets enable a level of privacy that is simply impossible on the Internet.

■ *The Web* Intranets allow you to set up your own private 'Web', using Web servers to make available Web-based pages to intranet members only (chat, Usenet and e-mail facilities are also available).

■ *E-mail management* Intranets help to limit the quantity of internal e-mail messages generated, as internal departments can set up their own Web pages so information can be provided without the need for e-mail.

▓ *Cost* A lot of Internet software is either free or very cheap and the freeware on offer includes Apache (one of the leading Web servers) and various e-mail software programs.

Although it is possible to set up a company intranet that has no connection to the Internet, connecting to the Net allows for greater flexibility.

However, if your intranet connects to the Internet, you need to take the issue of security very seriously. The type of information that passes between the Internet and your intranet has to be carefully controlled. To do this, you will have to set up a firewall (named after the barrier that protects a car's passenger compartment in the event of an engine fire).

A firewall will protect the information within the intranet from external users. It can also help you restrict Internet access to e-mail only.

There are several Internet sites where you can find out more about intranets. Here are three of the best:

▓ *Firewalls FAQ www.interhack.net/pubs/fwfaq* This site provides answers to all your firewall questions.

▓ *Intranet FAQ www.innergy.com/ifaq.html* Answers to frequently asked questions relating to intranet technology can be found here.

▓ *HarrierZeuros www.harrier.com* This UK-based site includes sections on intranets and firewalls.

Figure 9.1 *HarrierZeuros provides advice on intranets from a UK perspective*

summary

The free flow of communications within your business should be nurtured and encouraged. If e-mail use is too tightly controlled, you could end up missing out on the many benefits e-mail can offer within your organisation.

This said, as e-mail is still a relatively new communication tool, people may need guidance on how to use it effectively. E-mail, and the Internet in general, need to be used carefully by employees in order to maintain the reputation of your business. E-mail policies, intranets and firewalls will provide you with effective ways of protecting internal communications. Rather than being seen just as precautionary measures, however, they should be used to strengthen the sense of community for your employees, facilitating more open interaction.

glossary

The world of e-business is made more intimidating by the amount of jargon that surrounds it. Here are the words you are most likely to come across during your online efforts. The names of the main e-business players are also incorporated.

address book   A directory in a Web browser where you can store and manage e-mail addresses.

ADSL   Asymmetric Digital Subscriber Line. A high-speed, high 'bandwith' (see below) telephone line.

article   The name given to a single message posted to a newsgroup.

attachment   A file added to an e-mail to be sent via the e-mail system.

audience   Refers to each individual section of your online public. Each business has various audiences (customers, investors, journalists and so on).

B2B   Business to business.

B2C   Business to consumer.

bandwith   The capacity of the fibre-optic cables that carry information. The higher the bandwith, the faster information will pass through a cable.

banner ad An online advertisement in the form of a band of text and graphics. Banner ads generally contain a hypertext link to the advertiser's site.

Berners Lee, Tim Conceived the Web in 1989 as a tool for sharing information via his invention of HTML. Now he is Director of the World Wide Web Consortium (W3C).

Bezos, Jeff Founder and CEO of Amazon.com.

binaries Files attached to newsgroup articles, usually in the form of images or zip files.

bookmark A bookmark is a software tool that automatically loads the page it refers to.

bps (bits per second) The higher the number, the faster the speed of the modem.

bricks and clicks Refers to an integrated offline/online approach.

bricks and mortar A phrase used to evoke the 'real world'.

bricolage Claude Levi-Strauss, the French anthropologist, refers to bricolage as the act of creating things from whatever is lying about. Many people use the term to describe the opportunistic way in which the Web is put together.

broadband High-bandwith technology that is revolutionising the way the Internet is used by businesses and consumers.

browser Software that allows you to access the Internet and World Wide Web. Internet Explorer and Netscape Navigator are the most commonly used browsers.

bulletin board Software that provides an e-mail database where people can access and leave messages.

C2C Consumer to consumer.

cancel option   Useful in mail and newsgroup systems. Allows you to delete a message before or just after posting an e-mail message or newsgroup article.

Case, Steve   CEO of AOL.

chat   An interactive conversation occurring in real time on the Web. *See* chat system.

chat system   Enables users to have an interactive, typed conversation. Chat systems therefore build an online network of people who interact not just with the Web page but with other users as well.

clicks and mortar   *See* bricks and clicks.

click-through   The act of clicking on a link to be transported to another site. The term is most commonly used in the context of banner advertising.

community   A group of Internet users with a shared interest or concept who interact with each other in newsgroups, mailing-list discussion groups and other online interactive forums.

content services   Sites dedicated to a particular topic.

crawler   A type of search engine 'robot'.

cross-posting   The act of posting the same messages into several different news or discussion groups simultaneously.

cyberspace   Term originally coined in the sci-fi novels of William Burroughs to refer to the online world and its communication networks and to evoke its intangible sense of space.

distribution list   A list of e-mail addresses given one collective title. You can send a message to all the addresses simultaneously by referring to the list title.

domain name   The officially registered Web site address of your site.

dot bam   Dot 'bricks and mortar'. A real-world business with a strong Web presence.

dot.com   Used to refer to a company based exclusively online.

download   The term used to describe the transfer of a computer file from a server to a PC or Mac.

e-business   The catch-all term for the business world online. It also signifies an individual online business or company.

e-commerce   Business transactions over the Internet.

e-mail   Electronic mail. A message sent across the Internet, or the act of transferring messages between computers, mobile phones or other communications connected to the Internet.

e-mail system   The collective e-mail software systems that allow you to create, send and receive e-mail messages.

e-media relations   The practice of building relationships with editors and journalists via the Internet, especially when they work for the e-media.

e-media release   An online interactive, press release sent via the e-mail system.

emoticons   Common symbols used in e-mail and newsgroup messages to denote particular emotions by resembling faces on their side. :-) therefore indicates happiness (a smiley face), while :-(conveys unhappiness (an unhappy face). The word 'emoticon' is a hybrid of 'emotion' and 'icon'.

e-TV   Interactive television, accessed via a computer or a TV set.

e-zines   Online interactive magazines that only exist on the Internet.

filter   Software that can discriminate between types of incoming and outgoing e-mail messages.

flame   A 'heated' and hostile message posted in a newsgroup, usually in response to spam (see entry under 'S'). Also, the act of posting such a message.

form   A means of collecting data on Web pages using text boxes, radio buttons and other facilities. Forms are used as a way of making sites more interactive as well as for sales and marketing purposes.

forums   Newsgroups, mailing-list discussion groups, chat rooms and other online areas that allow you to read, post and respond to messages.

freeware   Free software programs.

FTP   file transfer protocol. This is the standard method of uploading content from your computer to your server.

Gates, Bill   Microsoft's founder Chairman. Although slow to appreciate the importance of the Internet, Gates has converted Microsoft into a company aiming to write the code for the next generation of Net-compatible devices.

GIF   graphic information file. Used on the Internet to display files that contain graphic images.

groupware   A set of technology tools enabling businesses to share software.

history list   A record of visited Web pages you can access via your browser. It can help you find sites you haven't been able to bookmark.

hit counters   Software that records the numbers of hits for a site.

hits   A hit is a transfer from a server to a browser. Each time a browser transfers a text page that has no graphics, that represents one hit. If the page has a graphic inside it, that's two hits. If it has two graphics, that's three hits, and so on. Hits, therefore, do not provide an accurate measurement of the number of times your Web site has been visited.

homepage   The first and/or main page on a Web site.

host   A company that holds your site on its server.

host computer   This is simply a computer connected to the Internet.

HTML   Hypertext Mark-up Language. A computer code used to build and develop Web pages.

hyperlinks   *See* hypertext links.

hypertext links   Generally found on Web pages (although they can be used in e-mail messages), hypertext links link to HTML pages and documents.

hypertime   The fast-moving pace of the Internet, as well as the decentralised nature of online time.

information overload   The situation of having so much information on your site as to bore or intimidate your customer.

Internet   The global network of computers accessed with the aid of a modem. The Internet includes Web sites, e-mail, newsgroups and other forums. This is a public network, though many of the computers connected to it are also part of intranets. It uses Internet protocol (IP) as a communication standard.

intranet   Internal, private computer networks using Internet technology to allow communication between individuals within organisations.

IRC   Internet Relay Chat. *See* chat.

ISP   Internet service provider. A firm that provides Internet services, such as e-mail and Web hosting facilities.

itchy-finger syndrome   A slang reference to Internet users' hunger for interactivity.

junk mail   *See* spam.

keywords   Words used by search engines to help find and register sites.

kill file   An instruction used in a newsgroup by your newsreader to skip particular articles, according to criteria you specify.

links   Text or graphic icons that move you to different Web pages or sites. Links are activated by clicking on them with a mouse.

list server   Software that runs a mailing list.

log on/off   To access/leave the Internet.

lower-level domain   The main part of the domain name. For most e-business sites, this is usually the company or brand name.

lurk   To read messages in newsgroups or mailing-list discussion groups, but not post anything yourself.

mail server   A remote computer (usually your ISP) enabling you to send and receive e-mail.

mailing list   A collection of e-mail addresses.

McNealy, Scott   Chairman and CEO of Sun Microsystems. Played an instrumental role in the shaping of the Internet.

m-commerce   mobile commerce. E-commerce via mobile phones using WAP and other technologies.

META tags   The keyword and description commands used in your Web page code to help search engines index your Web site.

moderator   Someone in charge of a newsgroup, mailing list, discussion group or similar forum. The moderator censors any unwelcome messages.

modulator/demodulator   More commonly known simply as a modem, this is an internal or external piece of hardware plugged into your PC or Mac. It links into a phone socket, enabling computer-based information to be transmitted over a phone network.

multi-phased medium   A medium, such as the Internet, that can be used in different ways for different ends.

navigation   The way a visitor travels or is directed around a Web site via links.

Net   Short for the Internet.

Net-head   Internet-obsessed individual.

netiquette   The etiquette of using the Internet. It is mainly used in the context of e-mail and newsgroup communication.

newbie   Slang term for a new newsgroup member.

news reader   Software enabling you to search, read, post and arrange newsgroup messages.

newsgroups   Collectively referred to as the 'Usenet', newsgroups are online discussion areas, each centred on a subject of common interest. People post messages to the groups that all the other members can read. There are over 40,000 active newsgroups on the Internet, covering topics as diverse as social welfare reform and South Park.

niche   A narrow but unified market or audience segment. The Internet is particularly suited to niche markets and audiences.

NNTP   Network News Transport Protocol In newsgroups, NNTP is the method by which newsreader software communicates with news servers across the Internet.

offline   Any activity or situation that does not involve being connected to the Internet.

online   The state of being connected to the Internet via a modem.

operating system   Software stored in a computer that controls hardware components and processes that run on them.

P2P   Peer-to-peer. Technology that allows Internet users to download compressed files from other users. Can also stand for 'path to profitability', which investors look for in new Internet start-ups.

plain text   Text that is encoded and contains no layout information, non-HTML text.

post   the act of sending an article to a newsgroup.

rank   A search engine position.

real world   Everything outside the Internet.

refresh   The act of reloading a Web site page or the whole site.

robot   A tool used by search engines to find and examine Web sites.

search engine   A site that enables you to conduct a keyword search of indexed information on its database. Also refers to the software used in this process.

secure server   Hardware and software that secures e-commerce credit card transactions so there is no risk of people gaining access to credit card details online.

signature (file)   Information appended to the end of a message that identifies the sender's details. You only need to write a signature file once and you can then attach it to your e-mails as often as you like.

silver surfers   Mature Internet users.

smiley   *See* emoticon.

snail mail   Net-head term for the real world's postal service.

snooze news   Company 'news' that will not interest journalists or editors.

spam   Junk mail on the Internet, normally in the form of unsolicited and unwelcome e-mail messages. This term is used most frequently in the context of newsgroups to refer to the process of posting the same article repeatedly to different newsgroups. The term is a reference to the famous Monty Python 'spam, spam, spam' sketch, where spam is served with everything.

spider   A type of search engine 'robot'.

sysop   Systems operator. *See* moderator.

system administrator   Someone responsible for the management of an e-mail system.

thread   An ongoing newsgroup topic.

top-level domain   The concluding part of a domain name, such as the .com or .co.uk suffixes.

traffic   The number of people visiting your site.

trolling   The act of posting a newsgroup article with the deliberate intent of provoking a heated, or 'flamed', response.

URL   uniform (or universal) resource locator. A full Web address – for example, http//www.yac.com.

Usenet   The system that distributes newsgroups. Also, this is the collective term for newsgroups.

visitors   The people who come to your Web site.

WAP   Wireless Application Protocol. The mobile equivalent of HTML.

Web master   Someone in charge of a Web site.

Web page   A single document stored at a Web site. A single Web browser window displays a single Web page at a time.

Web rings   Collections or communities of different Web sites and pages.

Web site   A collection of Web pages.

World Wide Web/Web   The World Wide Web does not mean the Internet. The World Wide Web is, in fact, a software system running across the Internet. It consists of (literally) billions of Web pages, usually containing text, images and HTML links.

Yahoo!   The world's most popular Web directory.